UNDERSTANDING
EDUCATIONAL
AIMS

COLIN WRINGE
University of Keele

London
UNWIN HYMAN
Boston   Sydney   Wellington

Published by the Academic Division of
Unwin Hyman Ltd
15/17 Broadwick Street, London W1V 1FP, UK

Allen & Unwin Inc.,
8 Winchester Place, Winchester, Mass. 01890, USA

Allen & Unwin (Australia) Ltd,
8 Napier Street, North Sydney, NSW 2060, Australia

Allen & Unwin (New Zealand) Ltd in association with the Port Nicholson
Press Ltd, 60 Cambridge Terrace, Wellington, New Zealand

First published in 1988

British Library Cataloguing in Publication Data

Wringe, C. A.
    Understanding educational aims.
1. Education – Aims and objectives
I. Title
370.11   LB17
ISBN 0–04–370172–8
ISBN 0–04–370173–8 Pbk

Library of Congress Cataloging-in-Publication Data

Wringe, C. A. (Colin A.)
    Understanding educational aims / Colin Wringe.
        p.   cm.
Bibliography: p.
Includes index.
ISBN 0–04–370172–8 (alk. paper). ISBN 0–04–370173–8 (pbk. : alk. paper)
1. Teaching.   2. Education – Aims and objectives.
3. Education – Philosophy.   4. Social values.   I. Title.
LB1025.2.W75   1988
370.11 – dc19   87–27078

Typeset in 11 on 12 point Garamond by Nene Phototypesetters Ltd
and printed in Great Britain by Billing & Sons Ltd, Worcester

Contents

For
William and Alison

Preface

It is a frequent remark that where an intending or, indeed, an established teacher does not shine or is positively falling short the reason may not always be simple classroom ineptness, still less a lack of detailed subject knowledge. Conscientious good intent may be there, and even a liking for children.

What so often fails is confidence in any long-term sustainable and at the same time clearly achievable purpose. Terms such as aimlessness, demoralization or anomie are too strong; automatism and lack of conviction are nearer the mark. In this regard, teachers have a problem not shared by most other professions. Doctors, businessmen, bricklayers and others will be in little doubt about what they are trying to achieve and not short of daily indications of how well they are succeeding. Press a teacher on these topics and the response will often be embarrassment or evasion.

Many teachers with the perspective of experience do, of course, have aims which they see themselves as fulfilling over time. But they keep fairly quiet about them. Possible educational aims are various and may be contentious. Expression of them may appear naive or bear the hubris of self-importance. No one wants to tempt Providence, or be thought guilty of preaching for the benefit of younger colleagues.

Tutors too may have reasons for reticence in the matter of aims. In the climate of Academe these days, whatever is not empirically demonstrable or in tune with a certain ideology is suspect. So aims are not discussed. We lose belief in their reality and their relevance, and find refuge in the routine of day-to-day objectives, or distant ideals which we may dream of but can do little to advance.

Such observations have been the motive for writing the present book, in which I attempt to review such earlier writings on aims as may be found and consider some more recent directions in educational policy. Writers on education are nowadays chary of acknowledging any particular discipline, but I have drawn heavily on the work of philosophers. The important task seemed to be to clarify what our aims should be, rather than simply discover how far they were endorsed by this or that section of the population.

My indebtedness to many writers will be obvious and, I hope, normally made clear. What is owed to discussion with students and colleagues can be less easily identified. I dare say, and readily acknowledge, that one or two who read what follows may sometimes come upon reflections that seem to belong to both, or even a whole group, of us.

I cannot conclude this preface without a special word of thanks to Philip Snelders, with whom I have worked on a number of projects over the years, and whose comments and encouragement in the writing of the present book have been most valuable.

CW

PART I

Introduction

Chapter One

Aims: Who Needs Them?

Why Should Teachers Concern Themselves with Aims?

If we ask what is presently the most serious shortcoming of the teaching profession, we shall almost certainly be told by many of Her Majesty's Inspectors, Local Authorities and politicians that it is that many of its members lack the necessary skills to do the job that is required of them. New teachers, and those older ones who have remained on the lower rungs of the promotion ladder, are supposed to lack certain 'classroom skills' while those whose ambitions have taken them further in their careers are held to lack the 'managerial skills' appropriate to the running of complex organizations.

This all sounds very modern and businesslike. The malaise is diagnosed in terms of the shortcomings of individuals. These will, of course, require much effort to put right, but do not demand any embarrassing reflections either on the general way we run our schools or upon what we are attempting to achieve by their means. Teachers must simply spend more time learning the supposed skills of the classroom and, incidentally, less time thinking about the nature, significance and social and political role of the lifetime's work on which they are about to embark.

No doubt there is much sense in all this. A teacher who cannot plan a sensible lesson at the right level for a particular group of pupils or devise a variety of tasks and activities that can be accomplished in the time-tabled forty minutes, or whatever, has something to learn. So has he if he cannot write quickly and legibly on the blackboard, or deal effectively with lively third-formers who insist on playing the fool. These are elementary parts of the teacher's stock-in-trade which all members of the profession must possess. It is doubtful, however, if all so-called 'ineffective teachers' and positively miseducative schools will be transformed by these means alone.

Where the educational experience being offered to pupils is unsatisfactory the problem may lie, not simply in clumsy or unskilled performances, but in the lack of any sense of what the point is in teaching a particular lesson, a particular subject or, indeed, in the educational enterprise as a whole.

No doubt it is naive to suppose that if only we get our aims straight, the rest will follow. But even this contains an element of truth. Skills are more readily acquired and more aptly applied when they are seen to be linked to some desirable end. Teachers undeniably need their armoury of knacks, dodges and elements of personal style acquired in the course of training and experience. But with equal urgency they also need a collectively acceptable rationale for the many activities and diverse aspirations in the pursuit of which they are engaged.

There is, of course, no single overriding goal which all of us engaged in the activity of education should be striving to achieve. On the contrary, there are many legitimate and proper aims which may be pursued under the aegis of education, and things often go most wrong when this fact is forgotten. It is therefore proposed to examine various candidates for the status of educational aims that are commonly advocated, or tacitly assumed.

The teaching profession, it will be suggested, needs to be in possession of a body of understanding of the educational enterprise and its various objects which, as far as possible, commands a measure of general consent among rational and responsible practitioners, in order to meet the requirements of principled co-ordination on the one hand, and an appropriate degree of self-direction on the other.

Life in the Classroom: Other-Direction and Self-Direction

Reference to self-direction may come as a surprise to many readers of this book. Those who have yet to undergo their first teaching experience in school may expect to receive fairly explicit instructions about what they are to do, even on a day-to-day basis, over the first few years. Their anxieties will be less about deciding what to do than about whether they will be capable of performing what is required of them by others.

Now it is certainly true that the teacher may be given a textbook whose content he is expected to transmit, and even told the rate at which it is to be transmitted. More likely than in the past, the individual teacher or even the whole department may be expected to follow a syllabus worked out by someone else – or by a committee of which the teacher may or may not have been a member.

In recent years both national and local inspectorates have taken to issuing curricular frameworks and subject guidelines. This has encouraged the impression of the education service as a hierarchical bureaucracy in which aims are expressed at the 'top', these being transmitted downwards as demands which are to be met by acts of compliance below. And, of course, the student on teaching practice will find his friendly neighbourhood head of department or class teacher ready to help him with the detailed planning of his first few lessons.

He will, however, probably be surprised to find how reluctant his older colleagues are to tell him what to do with any precision. Professional tutors are unlikely to articulate educational policies of general application. Their valuable and often very welcome advice is more likely to concern the amounts of time and energy to spend on preparation and marking, how to deal with awkward situations with particular pupils or other members of staff, what the local rules and practices are in relation to dress, movement and sanctions, and so on.

It is to be hoped that those drawing up curricular guidelines pay some heed to overall educational aims, but such guidelines offer little help in deciding which of many possible aims one ought to be giving emphasis to at a given time. Here and now, the teacher may need to decide whether a certain pupil should be treated rather sharply because his behaviour and perception of himself and others is no longer socially acceptable, given his head to develop his sense of personal autonomy, made to get down to some serious work for the sake of his vocational future, or encouraged to stop stuffing his head with facts in order to reflect upon his work in a more detached way. From a logical point of view, the notion that talking about aims is not very practical cannot be sustained. One cannot even begin to be practical or make sensible decisions about what one should be doing or how one should be doing it without some idea of what one is hoping to achieve. Practical activity, even of a simple kind, cannot be conceived of without the notion of an end in view.

This does not mean that teachers constantly have to spend a great deal of time discussing their aims with each other. Often these will be obvious enough. Also, part of the point of considering the question in depth in a detached way during periods of initial and in-service training is to ensure a measure of clarity and mutual understanding between members of the profession, so that fundamentals do not have to be constantly thrashed out *de novo* in the heat of a busy term.

The Scope of Educational Aims

Even people with such apparently clearly defined missions in life as policemen, doctors, prison warders and businessmen might gain more real benefit for themselves and others if more time were spent considering the ultimate purpose of their activities, rather than in achieving crude efficiency in the performance of their more immediate tasks. This is even more true for educators because of the far greater range of possibilities open to them. Doctors may choose between preserving life and preventing pain, businessmen between short- and long-term profit, and policemen between strictly enforcing the law and creating good community relations. But their options are relatively limited.

What teachers can achieve is restricted by what children are able or willing to learn, but the range of goals they may set themselves, and indeed have set themselves at various times, is almost limitless. There is scarcely any aspiration for good or evil which they cannot in principle seek to forward in the course of their work. Before considering a number of the more widely supported educational aims, however, it will be helpful to distinguish between the notion of an aim and two concepts with which it may easily be confused, namely that of an ideal and that of an objective. This is done not from sheer pedantry but because it is convenient to use these terms to refer to rather different things which, if not kept apart, tend to foul up discussion and obstruct the business of tackling the issues which really concern us. Our interest is in aims rather than in either ideals or objectives and the drawing of clear distinctions between them will enable us to exclude these latter from our discussion at this early stage.

Aims Are Not Ideals

No doubt many, if not most, people have ideals of some sort, be these the ideal home for one's retirement, the ideal marriage partner or the ideal society in which all are equal, free and well cared for. This, in itself, is obviously no bad thing. If the alternative is self-satisfaction and complacency, let us have ideals by all means. The problem is that the terms 'ideal' and more especially 'idealist' have managed to get themselves a bad name, for a number of reasons.

For some, an idealist has become synonymous with an impractical dreamer who thinks the ideal world he yearns for is already with us, or is just around the corner, and consequently fails to protect the practical interests of himself and those who depend on him. A teacher whose ideal was an educational system without examinations and, as a result, failed to help his pupils gain the qualifications they needed for the jobs they eventually wanted to do, or the advanced courses they hoped to follow, would be an 'idealist' of this sort.

Sometimes the term 'idealist' may be used to refer to reformers, politicians and other dedicated individuals who pursue their ideals of religious dedication, artistic achievement, truthfulness or social justice regardless of the cost in suffering to those around them.

So much for those who are sincere in their idealism. The other side of the coin is that many people may, in some sense, possess or hold ideals without this actually having much effect on what they do. This, no doubt, is a harmless, much satirized and largely inoffensive foible. More trouble is caused by the variant of this species who not only has ideals but will not shut up about them, and who gives himself airs on the strength of them, as if uttering virtuous ideals entitled one to the same degree of respect as a life actually devoted to virtuous conduct. The 'idealistic' ex-teacher who despises his former colleagues for 'compromising' over mixed ability teaching when he himself has escaped from the classroom would be an example of this.

Aims and ideals have often been confused by those who write

7

about education, and this has led to much misunderstanding. It has been largely responsible for the unpopularity and even embarrassment that tends to surround the discussion of aims, and this in turn has led to a number of important questions remaining unexamined.

The significant feature of ideals is not that they cannot be reached. Indeed, it will be argued that our most important aims are such that they may not be susceptible to complete fulfilment. It is rather that, being the embodiment of perfection in an imperfect world, their espousal readily lays one open to the charge of being a fool, a fanatic or a hypocrite.

This is not the case with aims, at least in the sense in which I propose to use the term. Aims may be either good or bad. To corner the market in an essential drug in order to increase one's firm's profits is as much an aim as is the promotion of, say, adult literacy. Aims may be modest, or they may be ambitious. A teacher may aim to bring about a small improvement in the oral communication skills of a notoriously sullen group of fourth-formers. The aim – and I mean the aim, not the ideal – of a particular organization may be to promote the cause of equal educational opportunities. To be guided by aims implies neither impracticality nor insensitivity to the aims, interests or wishes of others. Aims are not dreamy visions of a distant state which we may or may not be doing something to bring about. Typically, they may be pointed to as explanations of actual conduct, providing the rationale for a particular action or activity. The conduct or activity is made sense of as a positive and deliberate step in achieving the aim in question, and clarification of a group's or an individual's aims, far from being impractical, may well be the first step in improving efficiency.

Aims may be pursued ruthlessly, but they may also be pursued prudently and in a spirit of compromise and consideration for the interests and legitimate aspirations of others. To compromise over an aim does not imply the same moral falling short as compromising over an ideal, nor do aims run the risk, as do ideals, of excusing conduct which we should otherwise recognize as unacceptable.

One may, of course, be as hypocritical about one's aims as about one's ideals. If an eminent politician visits South Africa his aim may be to crusade against apartheid, or it may be to capture his country's liberal vote in the next round of elections. But to state one's aims truthfully and to urge others to join one in promoting them is less offensive than parading one's ideals and implying some moral inferiority in those who do not share them.

If this evident distinction between aims and ideals has been blurred in the field of education, it is partly because certain writers, who were not invariably classroom teachers (Russell, 1926; Whitehead, 1929; Dewey, 1916, ch. 8), presented what were, on our understanding of the term, educational ideals under the slogan of 'The Aims of Education'. This was sometimes done in a rather insensitive way. Consequently, certain perfectly valid criticisms of existing practice and existing conceptions of the teacher's task – as lacking imagination and breadth of vision – were perceived by many practising teachers as personal criticism by people who were in an authoritative position but had little actual experience of what they were talking about.

Along with this must be considered the contribution of a certain ideology of the teaching profession prevailing in institutions of teacher education, many of which had originally been religious foundations. According to this ideology, teaching was less a profession than a 'vocation' demanding unbounded dedication, patience and love for one's unwashed and ragged pupils, equalling the love of the saint for his own personal colony of lepers.

Lectures on 'aims' often tended to be little more than harangues, a dose of 'uplift' to inoculate aspiring teachers against the discouragement of the real world of the classroom. In many institutions this was the prevailing perception of 'philosophy's' contribution to teacher preparation and educational thought. Rightly this was seen as, at best, an indication that the tutors involved were out of touch with the real world and, at worst, a form of moral bullying, an attempt to present the real problems of the classroom as personal shortcomings of the individual teacher, and to extract from the teacher a degree of dedication that was unreasonable.

Aims Are Not Objectives

A second important distinction to be made is that between aims and objectives. In everyday speech these terms may be more or less synonymous, except perhaps that the term 'objective', which has been made popular in the jargon of military strategy and management science, may be used when one wishes to give the impression of being particularly scientific or precise about what one expects to achieve. In educational discussion 'objectives' usually refers to specific pieces of learning which we intend to see achieved at the end of a piece of classroom activity, a particular lesson or number of lessons, or even at the end of a longer unit of work.

According to one widely held view of educational planning, both at the level of planning an individual lesson and in designing a whole curriculum, it is essential to begin one's deliberations by 'specifying one's objectives' (see, for example, Davies, 1976). That is, we must begin by saying *precisely* what we want our pupils to know, understand or be able to do or say at the end of the lesson, at the end of the term or whatever. Some writers (Popham, 1970; Mager, 1962) go further and claim that to spell out our objectives in terms of what our pupils know or understand is not sufficiently precise. What people 'know' or 'understand', they suggest, is rather vague and cannot be absolutely ascertained. Such writers claim that we should spell out our objectives not in terms of such vague and 'unscientific' notions as knowledge, understanding, sensitivity and so on, but in observable 'behavioural' terms. What do we want our pupils to be doing? How do we want their behaviour to be changed as a result of attending our lesson or following our syllabus?

· It is not proposed to enter deeply into the debate over how far educators' objectives need to be operationalized in a behavioural, observable way. A more moderate view is that many of the teacher's most important objectives are to be spelled out in terms which are internal to the pupil – his knowledge, understanding, emotive responses, sympathies and so on.

In many respects, recent emphasis given to the need for teachers and others involved in education to be specific about their objectives has been extremely beneficial. When this approach is accepted and applied it gives the business of lesson preparation and other levels of educational planning a quality of rationality and professionalism it may not always have had in the past. Once objectives have been identified, lesson planning becomes a matter of selecting the best and, in terms of time, effort and other resources, the most economical means of achieving them. Such an approach is valuable in stressing that teachers are not only supposed to perform in front of their classes for a certain length of time, keeping them amused or occupied, but are actually supposed to deliver the goods in terms of certain specific learnings which can, in principle and in fact, be checked up on.

This at least has the merit of transforming the teacher from a rather low-level comedian and child-minder into someone with a potentially useful job to do. His performance is to be judged not in terms of such intangibles as his appearance, manner, 'classroom presence', 'authority' or what have you but – due allowance being made for the nature of his particular class – on the basis of his actual achievements. Needless to say, these are not limited to anything so crude as examination passes but include everything that he succeeds in getting his pupils to learn. There is no reason to doubt that, class for class, some teachers succeed in getting their pupils to learn a great deal more than others. If the teacher's task is viewed in this light it would not be surprising if greater effectiveness is achieved by seeing one's lesson plan not in terms of 'finishing off Chapter 3' or 'doing *The Ancient Mariner*', but in terms of the specific learnings to which the reading of Chapter 3 or the study of the poem in question are intended to lead. If, in addition, we identify for ourselves the formal or informal tests by which we shall attempt to assess our performance in achieving our objectives, this will no doubt concentrate our minds wonderfully.

A further advantage of actually identifying our objectives as part of our planning is that it forces us to think about the things we expect our pupils to learn. It enables us to ask ourselves such questions as whether these are things we can reasonably expect to achieve with this group at this time (e.g. last period on Friday afternoon), whether they are appropriate to this group, or whether certain other objectives are not more urgent, would not be more worthwhile, or do not need to be achieved before our present objectives can be attempted.

This said, it must be conceded that not all educators are equally happy with the above characterization of the educational process as something more or less exclusively planned in terms of the setting and achieving of highly specific objectives, even where the notion of an objective is liberally interpreted as the development of knowledge and understanding, rather than simply as observable behaviours (Davies, 1976, pp. 65–9).

The insistence on identifying specific objectives in advance, with its suggestion of managerial professionalism, rational planning and accountability, may create a certain air of efficiency and indeed lead to improvements in the quality of many pupils' learning. But it has not been shown that objectives are the only thing to be taken into account in guiding and managing the educational enterprise. In

11

particular, it is not obvious that this way of looking at things takes sufficient account of the nature and complexity of human learning and human development and of the random and incalculable way this sometimes takes place. To many, such an approach seems too conscious and to embody too obvious a notion of teacher direction.

When we think of really successfully educated people it is difficult to see their most important qualities and characteristics as being the result of the mere accumulation of a large number of separate, consciously identified, individual items of learning. We are more likely to think of them as the result of people's having spent their formative years in a certain kind of environment, physical and social, in which certain values are manifest and certain desirable and stimulating activities undertaken.

Such a school environment would by no means be the result of a laissez-faire or haphazard style of management but would require great care, judgement and planning in the allocation of effort and resources. In such a school, in addition to formal classroom lessons one might expect pupils to have the opportunity of taking part in such activities as concerts and drama productions, a variety of sports and competitive events, expeditions, foreign language exchanges, social service, work experience and so on. Few would doubt that such activities contribute to the educational work of the school. Yet few would attempt to spell out beforehand the specific changes which participation in these activities was supposed to bring about in the understanding, character and competence of specific, named, individual children.

Nor should we fall into the trap of drawing too sharp a distinction between the supposedly formal work of the classroom and what takes place 'out of school'. It is perfectly possible to think of valuable learnings of a kind analogous to those mentioned above occuring as the result of taking part in a science or history project, reading a novel or discussing a mathematical problem without it being possible to foresee all the important learnings of all one's pupils in advance.

The words and actions of an effective teacher at a particular time will only partly be explained by the objectives specified for the lesson he is currently conducting. That he is at pains to correct a particular pupil's mistake or pass on a particular piece of information may relate to the objectives of this lesson. But he will scarcely allow misunderstandings to pass without comment, or good opportunities for feeding in important information to go unused simply because they do not relate to today's lesson objectives. Also, the manner of correcting or giving information, the relationship he establishes with his class and the way in which the content of his teaching is presented will reflect educational considerations which are not conveniently characterized in terms of lesson or even course objectives.

The teacher's current objectives, furthermore, cannot be the ultimate guide of his conduct, for if that were the case we should not be able to understand why these objectives should be chosen rather than others. The choice of one's objectives themselves must obviously be governed by further considerations of another kind.

The point of the above discussion has not been to deny the importance of being clear about what one is trying to do, or of avoiding self-deception about what one is achieving. Teachers do need to think about the specifics of some of the things they are attempting in a particular lesson or unit and even perhaps set themselves minimum targets for their classes as a whole. Our purpose has been rather to argue that it is not enough to think in terms of certain finite, clearly defined objectives if our understanding of the work of teachers and educational institutions is not to be unduly limited and impoverished. For it would indeed be a mediocre institution in which teachers only sought to achieve such things as could be specifically laid down beforehand, either by themselves or by their curriculum makers.

It has been necessary to emphasize this point somewhat to counterbalance the influence on educational thinking of writers whose enthusiasm for a particular mode of educational planning and, more generally, for the scientific management of institutions has led them to disvalue the notion of aims as being too unspecific for their purposes, and thereby to lose sight of a dimension of thinking not readily amenable to analysis in other terms.

So, Aims Are – ?

It is important to note that aims are not simply objectives writ large (cf. Davies, 1976, pp. 11–16). One might be tempted to think that if the *objective* of this French lesson is to teach, say, how to ask the way to various places in the language, the *aim* of the course as a whole must be to cover the whole list of linguistic functions

13

necessary to gain a good grade in the GCSE. By a similar confusion, if one thinks that objectives, aims and ideals differ not in their nature and logic but in mere magnitude, and the distance to be travelled for their achievement, one might go on to think that the French teacher's *ideal* was to teach all the grammar and lexis necessary to enable his pupils to speak the language with native accuracy.

Ordinary language does, of course, sometimes use 'aims' in this way, to mean a fairly distant sort of goal that is nevertheless finite and intended to be achieved by a certain date. We might say 'our aim is to collect £2,000 this year for the repair of the church roof'. Societies and political organizations may be set up for purposes which they describe as their aims, after the achievement of which they may cease to exist.

If all aims were of this kind, however, there would be no purpose in distinguishing them so carefully from objectives. For our purposes the essential logical feature of aims is that, by contrast with objectives, they are of an open-ended, on-going kind. The aims of the NSPCC or Amnesty International are to promote certain general improvements in the conditions of those in whose interests they are set up, or to protect such people from further abuse. It is to be hoped that the condition of children and political prisoners will gradually improve, but it is scarcely to be envisaged that child abuse and political persecution will so entirely disappear that the two organizations in question will simply be able to tick off their abolition as objectives that have been achieved, and turn their attention to other matters. In the nature of things, the need for vigilance is bound to remain.

It must be stressed that the reason why these aims will never be completely achieved is not because they are distant or hard, but because of their open-ended nature. They are not the sort of things that can be finished off once and for all. Societies having the aim of promoting good causes such as encouraging the arts or scientific research are in the same position. It would be unintelligible to say 'Having now successfully accomplished the promotion of scientific research, there is nothing left for us to do and the society can now be dissolved.' Yet the promotion of scientific research is not an ideal. It is a thoroughly practical, feasible undertaking. Its pursuit requires neither perfection nor the pretence of it.

It will be readily seen that the undertakings of many individuals, groups and institutions throughout the world would be made nonsense of if this concept of a practical but on-going, non-finite aim were not available to us.

Aims and the 'Point' of Activities

Many teachers' aims will be closely connected with the point of the subject or activity they are engaged in teaching. Different teachers may, for example, be concerned to develop and extend their pupils' concept of number, increase their fluency, confidence and range of oral expression, promote responsiveness to literary works or improve their skill and precision in the handling of tools and materials. The aims of these teachers will no doubt include the fostering of interest in and commitment to the various values and standards implicit in these aims.

To understand what is taking place in their lessons it is not necessary to point to some extrinsic purpose on the teacher's part such as securing employment for his pupils or promotion for himself. These considerations may also be in his mind, and may help to explain why these subjects appear on the curriculum, as well as the degree of effort this teacher puts into his work. To use a hackneyed comparison: to explain why a basketball player moves to an unmarked position when his team-mate secures the ball, it is necessary to know that the aim or point of the game is to toss the ball into the opposing goal. It is less informative, even if perhaps not entirely irrelevant, to know that the player wishes to impress his girlfriend among the spectators and also, in general, to keep himself fit.

Besides being guided by the aims appropriate to their subject teachers will, of course, be attempting to secure certain particular objectives in each lesson. It will be clear from what has been said earlier that progress towards the achievement of the teacher's aims will not entirely consist of the sum of his achieved, pre-specified objectives. How one goes about achieving a particular objective, furthermore, will be constrained by one's underlying aims.

This lesson's objectives may include ensuring that a certain geometrical theorem is thoroughly learned, that the main content of scenes in the first act of *Macbeth* is known, that the method of making a dovetail joint is mastered. Conceivably these objectives may be most swiftly and efficiently achieved by means of rote learning and frequent testing with humiliating penalties for those who commit minor errors. But such an approach will be ruled out if it runs counter to more general aims, such as promoting an understanding of the subject or enthusiasm for it. A teacher who realizes this and modifies his teaching strategies accordingly is implicitly recognizing that aims as well as skills and objectives are of practical consequence in his teaching.

In addition to lesson and syllabus objectives and the aims inherent in teaching particular subjects, teachers may also think that their work is related to such larger purposes as developing the potential of individual pupils, contributing in various ways to the creation of a better world, promoting a commitment to certain intrinsically worthwhile activities, or the pursuit of such things as rationality and truth. Aims of this order are neither objectives nor ideals. They are implicit in much that takes place in schools, and help explain the spirit of seriousness with which education is often undertaken, and the passion with which educational issues are often debated.

Of course, such aims are inclined to sound rather grand and not at all the sort of thing one would want to be heard talking about in a crowded staffroom. Publicly, perhaps, it is as well to follow the fashion for seeming macho and hardbitten, to talk of A bands and C bands, of half-term dates and pension rights. But the question 'What are we doing all this for?' is not entirely idle or without practical implications.

Without reflection upon such questions we may either persist mindlessly in the established round, or be blown by every whim and educational fashion that comes our way. An understanding of our own aims is the *sine qua non* of both consistency and progression and may make the all-important difference between purposeful, effective teaching and desultory, pointless activity. However precise our specific objectives, it may be said that without some clear conception of our various aims, we simply do not know what we are doing.

Chapter Two

A Framework for the Discussion of Aims

Aims and Value Judgements

Our arguments for particular educational aims must necessarily involve more fundamental value judgements regarding such matters as the nature of the good life for the individual or society, the ways in which individuals ought to relate to each other, what goals it is in general desirable to pursue, and so on. Serious examination of these questions raises further ones, sometimes referred to as 'meta' questions, about the nature, validity and logic of value judgements themselves. It is neither possible nor desirable to consider these questions here, for to do so would take us away from the immediate educational context and into the realms of general philosophical controversy.

It may, however, be helpful to make explicit a number of assumptions in relation to value judgements which underlie much of what follows. It should be emphasized that none of these assumptions is regarded as definitive. Far less is it suggested that readers should themselves accept any of them without examination. The intention is not to advocate any particular ethical stance but simply to avoid misunderstanding by putting our presuppositions up for scrutiny at an early stage, rather than seeming to smuggle them in surreptitiously. Readers who wish to pursue the important issues they raise are referred to the various standard ethical works mentioned in the Suggestions for Further Reading on pp. 140.

To begin with the question of justifying ethical claims, it is here

17

presumed that, despite arguments surrounding the relationship between fact and value (Foot, 1967), we cannot argue from facts to policies in any straightforward way without referring to further value positions. For example, although there may be good empirical evidence for supposing that certain teaching methods produce slightly better academic results, this is not in itself a clinching argument for adopting those methods, for we can always ask: 'But is this small improvement in academic results really so important?'

It is also held that no one is in a position to 'see' or pronounce it as 'self-evident' that certain things are good and ought to be done without further ado. For those things which some insist on regarding as self-evident are often those which others find most contentious. If two people claim to 'see' the obvious desirability of two opposing courses of action, there is no means of judging between them, and discussion is of no avail. Yet if we differ with someone in the matter of values and sincerely wish to reach an understanding with them, discussion is our only recourse.

The ability to resolve at least some moral differences by rational discussion is also an indication that values are not purely matters of taste or subjective emotion. If one of us prefers strawberry and the other vanilla, rational discussion is not likely to make either of us change our minds, though irrational appeals to vanity or snobbishness might have some effect. But if we disagree about whether girls should be prevented from dropping mathematics in order to take up home economics, a thoughtful and attentive unravelling of the issues involved may prove profitable and enlightening to both of us. This is despite the fact that we may each start off with an emotional commitment to our original position and, though our positions may become closer, the ultimate weighting of values may not be possible to determine with precision.

The validity of certain aims is therefore not to be established simply by assembling more facts, even facts about the preferences of others. It cannot be directly intuited, or accepted on the authority of others who claim to intuit for us. Our views on these matters are not entirely subjective and discussion is of some avail. But on what positive assumptions may such discussion reasonably be based? This is a point upon which our argument is bound to seem vulnerable. For whenever a value judgement is asserted, further questions of justification may always be asked – a fact confirming rather than disproving the availability of value judgements to rational scrutiny. The result of this fact, however, is that whatever substantive assumptions we took to be fundamental, it might still be asked 'But why stop here?'

Consequently, it can only be tentative and provisional if we regard it as especially significant that, as far as we can conceive, human beings have but one life in which to achieve a satisfactory existence. The quality of that life depends partly on material circumstances, and partly on the quality of our understanding and learned capacities both to achieve and to enjoy. It appears to be the case that we get a better life on the basis of mutual understanding and co-operation with others than we should in isolation. For whatever reason, however, we do differ from each other in both our capacities and our preferences. There appears to be no reason to suppose that any one person's opportunities for achieving a satisfactory life should be regarded as any more or any less important than anyone else's.

These observations might seem to suggest that if *per impossibile* they were in a position to make such choices in advance, individuals would wish for an education that would enable them to secure a satisfactory life, however that might be defined. The same observations might also suggest that both social arrangements and educational undertakings that failed to recognize the moral independence and mutual non-subordination of individuals would be difficult to defend.

Both life and resources are finite and choices have to be made. Such choices may involve other equal and non-subordinate individuals and therefore require procedures of negotiation and justification within a social structure which is itself defensible. Since we are ourselves also non-subordinate, we have choices to make about how to live our own lives as well. There exists a range of activities, commitments and ways of life which others have found valuable. These, however, are not simply to be accepted as such without constant re-examination, or imposed upon others without their eventual understanding and approval.

Categories of Educational Aims

Some such assumptions as the above may suggest a form of crude categorization among the various aims which have, from time to time, been proposed by educational thinkers, namely:

(1) Aims which would confer benefits specifically upon the individual and favour his own ends and development.

(2) Aims concerned to preserve or bring about a desirable state of society.

(3) Aims to bring about such goals as the promotion of truth, rationality, excellence and so on which are sometimes held to be intrinsically desirable or worthwhile.

In recent years it has sometimes been suggested that aims in the second of the above categories, namely those of a social kind, are of particular importance (Hargreaves, 1982, pp. 77–160). Often, indeed, it is implied that other kinds of aims are in some way trivial or even politically suspect, serving as a means of protecting existing inequality and injustice. This, however, has rarely been the perspective of teachers or intending teachers and doubtless reflects the interests of influential groups within the academic hierarchy.

The question of priority among the various categories of aims may, of course, easily be avoided by saying that the three cannot be separated and that the distinction is more academic than real. One cannot promote the spread of knowledge without making at least some individuals more knowledgeable. A society whose citizens were well informed would be very different and, one hopes, better than one in which they were ignorant, and so on. This, however, is the answer of a politician rather than someone genuinely concerned with the clarification of issues and the pursuit of truth. It is naturally the case that in pursuing one of our sets of aims we often necessarily promote the others as well. But there are differences of emphasis and may, in fact, often be conflicts. White (1982, p. 20), for example, argues quite convincingly that the dedicated pursuit of certain kinds of excellence may be inimical, not only to the happiness but also to the proper all-round development of many individuals. Hargreaves (1982, pp. 77–112), arguing strongly for the priority of social aims, claims that our concentration earlier in the present century on the goal of developing the skills and capacities of individuals has led to social divisiveness, alienation and a widespread condition of anomie. No attempt will be made to resolve or disguise these conflicts, or suggest that any one category always has priority over the others. In considering the validity of any one educational aim it is always relevant to ask how far it is compatible with others, particularly if these latter appear to be exceptionally well grounded. In the absence of any final authority in the field of values, however, the question of which aims should have our final allegiance is necessarily contentious. Inspired leadership or official policy may serve to unify our efforts, but if these are to prove effective they must harmonize with prevailing teacher opinion rather than attempt to coerce it. For this reason, members of the teaching profession require a sophisticated understanding of the field of aims and their justification.

Needless to say, the nature of an aim under discussion necessarily determines the direction in which we must look for its justification. Those supposedly based on the good of individuals naturally direct us towards the question of how that good is to be conceived. Social aims, likewise, raise issues concerning the nature of a good society, as well as about the limits of the teacher's social role. Claims that certain activities or excellences are to be pursued 'for their own sake' are empty or rhetorical without some examination of the activities or excellences concerned.

Aims and the Concept of Education

Before turning to the task of examining educational aims in the three broad categories suggested above, there remains one further general point to clear up. This concerns the relationship between educational aims and discussion of the definition or so-called 'concept' of education.

It is, of course, tautologically true that for something to count as an educational aim it must be capable of being achieved in an educational context by recognizably educational means. It is also useful to distinguish between a range of responsibilities falling upon those employed as teachers which relate to the general welfare, safety and mental and physical health of pupils, and those centrally concerned with the development of their knowledge, understanding and other abilities and qualities of character as they pass from the condition of childhood to that of an adult. Resources and roles in society are, furthermore, allocated on the basis of some mutual trust and understanding as to how they will be utilized. Arguably, therefore, resources made available for educational purposes ought only to be employed in pursuit of ends which accord with some commonly accepted understanding of that term. To that extent, perhaps, definitions of education may be relevant to what a teacher's aims should be.

It is also useful on occasions to draw a distinction between related or contrasting concepts, as we have done in the case of aims, ideals and objectives, as a preliminary piece of clarification before proceeding to deal with substantive issues. There is a difference between telling a child to wipe his nose (and keep it wiped) and telling him to wipe his nose so as not to give his cold to others. In some educational discussions it may be helpful in getting someone to understand this difference, to begin by distinguishing between the notions of education and socialization. But how the child should actually be dealt with in a particular context will depend not on what one or other kind of treatment is called, but upon its likely effects, given the child's age, temperament and previous experience.

Likewise, the rightness or wrongness of what is done in the metalwork room does not depend on whether it is *called* education or vocational training but upon the desirability of turning pupils into capable and reflective individuals rather than simply transforming them into better workers.

All too frequently, however, concern with the concept of education is not a preliminary to further discussion but a means of bringing it to an abrupt close. Just when the argument about what teachers or schools should be trying to do is getting interesting, it seems to many students that this process is destroyed by the preremptory assertion that 'That isn't education, that is socialization/indoctrination/training' or whatever. A variant on this is the claim that 'This isn't what I/we/fluent speakers of English mean by education.' Sometimes, irritatingly and misleadingly, the authority of the Oxford English Dictionary or even Latin etymologies may be called upon to support these assertions.

In this connection reference may usefully be made to the well-recognized polemical device (Gallie, 1955–6; Naish, 1984; Montefiore, 1979) of defining certain 'honorific' terms in such a way as to deny their use to one's opponent. 'Education' is one such term. 'Democratic', 'Christian' and 'work of art' are others. If someone opposed to 'talk and chalk' teaching methods or the inclusion of vocational subjects in the curriculum denies that they are 'really' education he may hope to avoid having to show that talk and chalk methods are less effective than other approaches, or dodge the thorny question of how and when vocational skills are to be acquired.

It has long been understood (Hume, 1751, 3.I.i, pp. 507–20) that

22

questions about what ought to be done cannot be solved by studying the definition of terms. Confusion in this field among educators has been fostered, however, by a body of writing about educational aims which, despite John White's remarks to the contrary (1982, preface, pp. x–xi), may still retain some influence. Peters, in particular (1964, 1973b, 1973e; see also Hirst and Peters, 1970, pp. 17–41), spends much time in various analyses of the concept of education. According to these the term is supposed to apply to deliberately contrived learning procedures which (1) result in some form of betterment in the learner's character or state of mind, and (2) are morally acceptable and take place with the knowledge and assent of the learner. It is further specified that to qualify as education the learning must (3) in some way modify and extend the learner's cognitive perspective on the world, and (4) result in his disinterested commitment to certain intrinsically worthwhile pursuits.

That so much attention was given to the definition of education no doubt resulted from the philosophical assumptions of the preceding period when it was widely held that many of our philosophical problems would be resolved or simply disappear if only we gave some attention to the task of 'clarifying our concepts'. This particular analysis of education owes much of its influence to Peters' own personal charisma, as well as to its real value in rescuing educational theorists from the search for simplistic and crudely instrumental outcomes as educational aims.

Confusion arises because of the particular nature of these supposed criteria of education. It may or may not be true that 'betterment' is a criterion of education. But if it is, then it goes without saying that education is desirable, for betterment cannot be otherwise. It also goes without saying that pupils ought to be treated according to morally acceptable procedures, though whether these are limited to procedures that involve the conscious assent of pupils is a further question. More serious problems arise, however, when it is said (criteria 3 and 4) that education involves modifying pupils' cognitive perspective and securing their commitment to intrinsically worthwhile activities, particularly when these activities are identified with a specific set of disciplines and intellectual pursuits.

It will later be argued that there are indeed good reasons for extending a child's understanding of the world and encouraging his commitment to intrinsically worthwhile activities. This, however, is not because these things are part of a definition of education but because independent reasons can be given for thinking them desirable. In fairness it must be said that Peters himself has frequently emphasized the distinction between conceptual inquiry and substantive prescription. It is therefore the more ironic that his most influential work should have encouraged this confusion in so many of his followers.

Conclusion

Efforts to clarify a number of somewhat general issues in this chapter have been intended to enable our discussion of particular aims to proceed more constructively and with less hesitations than might otherwise have been the case. We are now in a position to turn to a critique of particular aims. It will be understood that in setting such considerations before intending and practising teachers our purpose is not to confuse or inhibit action, as is sometimes said. On the contrary, it is to help teachers to guide and evaluate their own activities and, as is increasingly necessary in the present climate, to defend their professional undertakings against the often political and one-sided criticisms of others.

PART II

Aims and the Individual

Chapter Three

The Limits of Happiness

There is a widely held view that not only all educational activity, but all human activity whatsoever ought to be directed towards the maximization of human happiness in one way or another. Writers who take this view may have in mind not only the happiness of the pupil here and now or in the future, but also the happiness of others who will be affected by his actions. To this extent the aim of promoting happiness relates both to the pupil as an individual and to the wider educational goal of contributing to the production of a better world in which all will live happier lives. Barrow (1976, pp. 79–103) has also attempted to reinterpret aims connected with intrinsically worthwhile activities in terms of their contribution to happiness or satisfaction.

As an ethical theory utilitarianism has a number of strengths. First, it is profoundly egalitarian. In its classic statement the overall aim of conduct should be to promote the greatest good of the greatest number, and in calculating the sum of human happiness each is rigorously to count for one, and none for more than one (Williams, 1972, p. 36). Secondly, it has the advantage of being thoroughly down to earth in that it provides a ready antidote to humbug, such as rules and regulations which appear to exist for their own sake and serve no obvious purpose, or the pursuit of traditions and high ideals which not only produce no increase of human happiness, but actually make people miserable.

Thirdly, provided one does not look too critically, the theory appears to suggest its own modes of implementation. In educational terms, for example, it might suggest that teachers ought to be concerned both with keeping pupils, as far as possible, in a happy state now and with ensuring that they learn things that will enable them to achieve happiness or avoid misery later on.

It must also be said that many of the supposed problems of utilitarianism as an ethical theory are by no means as insurmountable as some critics pretend. There are, for example, supposed to be difficulties surrounding the question of whether and why present happiness should be sacrificed for the sake of happiness in the future, or vice versa. Yet it is fairly clear that neither is necessarily desirable. A few moments of happiness now are not worth a lifetime's misery later on, nor is a lifetime of drudgery to be paid for by a short period of happiness at the end of one's days. It is the overall happiness of one's life that the utilitarian considers. Of course, to look back in contentment on one's former sorrows and anxieties may in itself be a source of happiness, whereas to look back in misery on former happiness may give rise to additional bitterness, especially if the situation has been in any way of one's own making.

There are held to be problems about the *nature* of happiness. No one imagines that happiness is purely a matter of pleasant sensations, but being tucked up in bed with a hot toddy might come near to it, especially if the previous night had been spent trying to sleep on a park bench in the freezing rain with a toothache. But we might even be happy with the toothache if we had just inherited a million pounds or finished writing *War and Peace*. People can be miserable in spite of apparently having achieved all their desires, feelings of happiness can be chemically produced, perhaps even permanently maintained, and certainly feelings of wretchedness can be dulled in the same way. Happiness may be the result of temperament rather than objective facts. What may make one person happy may leave another unmoved. Happiness may be unmerited or illusory.

These contradictions are supposed to show that happiness is no one thing but a blanket term for various physical and mental states, some of which may be ethically neutral or even reprehensible. In fact, they merely show that a number of different things may contribute to someone's happiness and that different people may be made happy in different ways. Even if someone is happy for the wrong reason, as Oedipus may have been on his wedding day, it is not his happiness that we judge to be bad but the thought of the much greater unhappiness that awaits him round the corner.

A further objection is supposed to be in the alleged absurdity of

28

the 'hedonic calculus' and the idea of calculating the relative amounts of happiness or misery caused by this course of action or that. How, it is sometimes asked, do we compare the pleasure created by building a municipal opera house with that which would result from a reduction in the rates? What units are we to use, and so on? It is true that the language of Bentham, one of the main proponents of the utilitarian doctrine, does sometimes invite this criticism, but we need not follow him in looking for any sort of mathematical precision. Often it is perfectly obvious which course of action will produce the greater happiness, even when the happiness would result from dissimilar causes. When it is not perfectly obvious, we simply have a difficult judgement to make, and this might be so whether dissimilar sources of happiness were involved or not. Utilitarianism is said to be a form of 'naturalism'. The point of this objection is that we cannot argue from 'x will make people happy' to 'x ought to be done' unless we first assume some such general premiss as 'you ought to do anything that makes people happy'. This objection, however, rests on something of a misunderstanding of what is involved in saying that something will make someone happy. Happiness is not just any kind of physical or mental state, but is closely connected with people's wants and desires.

It is, as we suggested, just possible to say 'I have everything I want, but I am unhappy'. But there is something paradoxical about such a statement. The person may be suffering from some kind of medical condition producing melancholy or, more likely, has other desires which he is not fully aware of or cannot articulate. One famous, if often misunderstood, argument for holding that happiness is desirable is precisely that it is widely, or perhaps universally, desired (Mill, 1861, pp. 32–3). It is true that people sometimes desire things that are morally bad. We may, for instance, be greedy or vindictive, but part of the reason why these things are reprehensible is that they bring unhappiness to others, and maybe also to ourselves.

In a community in which everyone's wants are acknowledged to be of the same importance, the fact that someone wants something and will be made happy by it is, in the absence of countervailing considerations, a reason for seeing he gets it. The very least that can be said is that someone's happiness is a good among others. What is less clear is that it is the only or ultimate good, or that the maximization of happiness provides the only criterion to be considered in answering the question 'What ought people (including teachers) to do?'

The view that happiness should be our overriding consideration does, however, raise a number of objections which cannot be disposed of quite so easily as those noted so far. One of these is the fact that sometimes there seems to be a fairly clear conflict between what will bring most happiness, or avoid most misery, and what ought to be done in the light of other considerations. Supposing, for example, the police were quite sure that someone was a criminal – a child molester, say – but realized they had not sufficient evidence to secure a conviction. Many people would certainly doubt that the police ought to fabricate the necessary evidence, even though they would be preventing further assaults and a great deal of misery.

The stock utilitarian reply to this objection is that moral rules have to apply universally. We are not supposed, that is, to calculate the amounts of happiness and misery caused by this particular case alone but consider whether, in general, the fabrication of evidence by the police would be productive of greater happiness. People who take this view say they are concerned with rule utilitarianism rather than act utilitarianism. A similar strategy is used to cope with the notorious difficulty utilitarianism has in explaining the notion of individual rights. If two men were standing in the cold and one of them owned a coat, we should not think it right for the other to take it from him, even if this second man, unlike the first, did not have a very thick vest either, and was more likely to suffer from the cold. For though taking the coat would reduce the sum of misery, it would violate the owner's property right. Rule utilitarianism is intended to enable us to argue that the owner's property right should not be violated because in general respecting such rights is likely to lead to more contentment than the contrary. Similarly it is, in general, likely to do more good than harm if we insist that the police do not fabricate evidence to secure convictions.

This kind of move is flawed, however. The distinction between act and rule utilitarianism cannot be maintained since any act which itself promotes more happiness than misery can be brought under a rule which would have to satisfy a rule utilitarian but would still let in actions which many people would find morally dubious. 'Policemen should fabricate evidence if (but only if) they know the accused is guilty' and 'Property rights should be set aside whenever this produces an increase in happiness' would both be cases in point. In addition, the move from act to rule utilitarianism appears to introduce a consideration other than happiness according to which actions are to be judged – namely that of consistency with a rule.

A second problem for utilitarianism, especially in the context of justifying educational aims, is the fact that many people appear to be perfectly happy doing things for which, as educators, we cannot have much enthusiasm. It is also the case that many of the things we do regard as very worthwhile (such as academic study or artistic creation, for example) do not actually seem to make us happy, and may even be accompanied by feelings of wretchedness (Elliott, 1977, p. 12). On the basis of mere pleasure, there would appear to be no reason for regarding such edifying activities as the reading of poetry as any more valuable than playing push-pin or any similarly trivial pastime. One move the utilitarian could make would be to concede that there is indeed no reason to prefer poetry. But this would be most unhelpful to the educator who has to prefer the human being who is dissatisfied with himself and strives to improve, to Mill's pig (1861, p. 9) who is perfectly satisfied to wallow where he lies.

Mill's own solution is to propose that there are different kinds of happiness, some of which are in some sense higher or better than others. This cannot simply mean that some forms of happiness are more intense than others and therefore count for double (say) in the hedonic calculus, for the happiness of the gambler may not be any less intense than that of the scientist or the creative artist. What Mill appears to mean is that some forms of happiness, such as those produced by more intellectual activities, are in some sense better or more worthwhile than others.

The problem is that Mill, rather like the rule utilitarian but in a much more obvious way, has introduced a new criterion of value into the argument – namely that of 'worthwhileness' or what-ever other quality it is that is supposed to distinguish one kind of happiness from another. In a sense he is perfectly right to do this, for though happiness is certainly a good, it is by no means the only good. But to make this move is to abandon the utilitarian position that the good is simply that which is pro-ductive of happiness.

From an educator's point of view it would seem clear that happiness, both now and in the future, must be taken into account. We do right and are not just being a 'soft touch' when we have regard to the happiness of our pupils, even when it conflicts with other aims. An educational system that kept pupils in unnecessary fear and misery on the grounds that they learnt better that way would be unconscionable. This would lead us to condemn a form of education which simply turned pupils into high achievers who could take pleasure in nothing but their own achievement and who were, in consequence, incapable of relating to others, led wretchedly competitive lives, or constantly inflicted misery on those around them.

On the positive side, one justification for equipping pupils with vocational and other qualifications might be that this would increase their chances of happiness by enabling them to follow the kind of occupation they wanted to follow. We must, however, be careful with this argument for, as will be suggested later (pp. 65–7), too great a concentration on vocational learning may limit rather than widen someone's range of options. If it is true that greater prosperity leads to greater happiness and that a more highly qualified workforce produces greater prosperity, that too might reasonably influence our educational programme.

It may also be a proper aim for teachers to have, that pupils should be able to become absorbed in the various activities they undertake and derive some pleasure from them, both in school and elsewhere. This need not be just a motivational strategy but a perfectly valid ground for teaching in such a way that pupils develop positive attitudes towards activities which others have found particularly rewarding.

Utilitarianism cannot rightly be accused of justifying an education designed to gentle the mass of pupils to accept exploitive drudgery in later life. Possibly, if people were absolutely certain to lead a life of drudgery, it might be better for them to do so with contentment, rather than in a state of bitterness and frustration – but even this is contentious. No utilitarian, however, need approve of a form of complacent contentment that merely aimed to prevent the drudge from throwing off his servile condition and demanding a more positively satisfying way of life.

Despite these points in its favour, utilitarianism ultimately remains inadequate, both as a moral doctrine and as a source of educational aims. There are many qualities and achievements we value and admire without paying too much attention to the amount of happiness they promote. In educational terms, promoting the happiness of children has much in common with other so-called child-centred aims. Though we are not entitled to disregard the happiness of our pupils and others, the doctrine provides us with few specific indications of the qualities and achievements educators should seek to pass on.

Is utilitarian a barren philosophy?
true like citizens charter approach

Chapter Four

Natural Growth, Needs and Interests

In the tough managerial atmosphere of our decade the aims of child-centred education often appear irrelevant and naive. The Plowden Report's humane insight that 'At the centre of the educational process lies the child' is nowadays usually referred to only for the purposes of ridicule (Straughan and Wilson, 1983, p. 17). Research, showing some teaching styles to be marginally more effective than others (Bennett, 1976), is often construed to suggest that teachers who consider themselves child-centred are professionally inferior to those who are more hard-boiled and coercive.

The slogans of child-centred education have presented an easy target to philosophers, more interested in demonstrating their analytical versatility than in identifying good practice. That these slogans contain incoherences cannot be denied. Yet they express important educational aspirations which happily continue to guide the work of at least some teachers. It is hoped that this positive contribution of child-centred educational theory will emerge from our discussion of the following three slogans, which may be taken as characteristic expressions of child-centred aims, namely:

(1) The teacher should foster the *natural growth* of his pupils and not impose his own (or society's) arbitrary demands.
(2) 'In educating the young the child's *interests* should be our principal guide.'
(3) What we teach should be determined by the child's present and future *needs*.

In discussing these three slogans, the first point to be made is that the child-centred ideology is best understood in terms of its opposite, the authoritarian or, as it was sometimes termed, the 'traditional' style of education, to which child-centred educators were so passionately opposed. In this connection it is important to note that the central feature of traditional education was not the old-fashioned and inhumane institutions in which it was supposed to be carried on, or even the repressive teacher–pupil relationships by which it was often accompanied. These were not, in themselves, the root of the problem but the consequences of an underlying philosophy.

Central to the approach to which child-centred educators were and, indeed, still are opposed is the assumption that what is to be taught is to be determined by some form of authority. Educational aims come from without. In some times and places this authority may be the governmental or religious hierarchy. A system in which the curriculum was centrally determined and schools were inspected to ensure that official guidelines were being followed would be a crude example of such an approach. Frequently the authority may have been that of social prestige, with the school attempting to emulate the aims of schools in the next category up the social ladder. But teachers who regard themselves as 'child-centred' may also be opposed to a situation in which the content of what is taught is determined in the light of what are conceived to be the logic and nature of certain intellectual disciplines, or the needs of society, without due regard to the nature of the child.

It is easy to see how aims received from without in this way might lead to conflict between teachers and their more high-spirited pupils. If the implementation of such aims is seen as the prime duty and obligation of teachers, then it becomes a test of their competence and machismo to bring this about with as little interference or delay as possible on account of anything pupils might want or have to say about it. Hence the so-called didactic style of teaching in which the teacher does all the talking, spends much of his time dictating notes, or writing on the blackboard, and in which the principle aim of classroom questioning and other forms of interaction is to ensure that pupils have been properly attending to what has been said. The task is not conceived as developing or extending anything the pupil may know or be interested in already, but as transferring knowledge from someone who is supposed to

35

know everything, to those who are credited with knowing nothing at all.

Needless to say, a them-and-us relationship and a whole repressive style of discipline may be associated with such an approach, especially if it is implemented by teachers with little social experience of handling others or little insight into how children tick or see the world. What is perhaps less widely recognized is that even where an apparently more humane relationship exists, where the teacher has a degree of charisma or charm, is good at jollying his class along by telling plenty of jokes and using more rewards than punishments, the essential feature of an approach in which aims come as given from without may still be present. Only the means employed are different.

It is in response to such a coercive, or at best manipulative approach that advocates of child-centred education have tended to drop into a rather horticultural idiom, speaking of the stunted, unnatural way of life to be found in many schools. Children, such writers may suggest, are naturally curious, kind, honest and intelligent. They love doing things such as painting, singing, reading, solving problems, exploring the world, working at practical tasks, and so on. We do not need to implant these things, the seeds are there already. All we need to do is to pro-vide the conditions in which they will develop naturally and in which the child will realize his own innate potential. There is, above all, no need for us to impose our own or society's arbitrary demands.

The image of organic growth may be contrasted with others such as those of forming or moulding the child into a useful artefact, filling him with good learning as if he were an empty pot or writing on the blank slate of his mind. Essentially, the child-centred educator assumes that by 'following nature' and simply 'fostering the child's natural growth' he, unlike the traditionalist, escapes the odium of imposing his own preferences on children. In effect he seeks to escape the responsibility for making value judgements or choices and decisions about the ends at which the educational process should be aimed.

Ultimately, however, such choices cannot be avoided, for the decision to 'follow nature' is as much a decision as any other, and merits the same scrutiny and debate. To suppose that we can decide what the ends of education are to be by studying child psychology and child development is to suppose that questions about ends can be settled simply by means of empirical studies aimed at bringing more facts to light.

This error is encouraged by certain ambiguities in our use of the word 'natural' and our misunderstanding of what is involved in growth when the term is applied to human capacities. As regards 'nature' there is a perfectly straightforward, value-neutral sense in which what is natural is simply what is there, or would be there but for human interference. What is, or is not, natural in this sense is a matter of fact. In contrast to this, however, especially since Rousseau and the Romantics, we have also used the word in a much more value-loaded sense, as the opposite of such terms as 'artificial', 'stilted', 'pretentious', 'forced', 'perverted', and so on. In this sense the word is used not just to describe, but to praise or advocate certain kinds of behaviour or action.

In the first of these senses we might say that nature is red in tooth and claw. The law of nature is the law of the jungle. The tape-worm and the scorpion are as much a part of nature as the dove and the rose. In certain situations rape, violence and egoism may be as natural as any other kind of conduct, if not more so. This, clearly, cannot be what the child-centred educator is advocating when he urges us to respect nature. For to say that something is natural in this sense is simply to describe the way things are, not to give a reason for preferring it. At the very outside, to say that something is 'only natural' in this sense may just help to excuse an action we might otherwise condemn.

Clearly, therefore, the advocate of natural growth must be thinking of nature in our second sense, in which calling something natural is not describing it but stating a preference. Presumably the qualities he wants to see developing naturally are those of intelligence, truthfulness, kindness, frankness, independence and rationality, rather than their opposites. But if you simply 'let nature take its course' in our first, value-neutral sense, either of these sets of qualities may develop, as may a mixture of the two.

There is a slight complication to this argument. A child-centred educator like Rousseau would probably reply that this second set of qualities (egoism, untruthfulness, servility, hypocrisy, violence and so on) are not natural at all, even in a purely descriptive sense.

On the contrary, they are actually produced by society; people are egoistic because society is competitive, untruthful because society is censorious, hypocritical and servile because society is hierarchical, and violent because they see violence around them.

Far from being natural to human beings these qualities are learnt in society. If society were not competitive, censorious, hierarchical, violent and so on human beings would be good, honest, kind and gentle. No doubt this is true, but not because these or any other moral qualities are inherent in human beings and would simply emerge if given the chance, but because they would be learnt, just as surely as bad qualities are learnt. For goodness, honesty, kindness and so on are just the qualities that would be practised and therefore available to be imitated in a society which was not competitive, censorious, hypocritical, hierarchical or violent.

No doubt it is the achievement of many child-centred educators to have produced for a time in their schools just such a community. But to do this takes blood, sweat and tears, and not a little skill. Such things do not just happen naturally. The educator deliberately creates such a community as a means of achieving the educational aims he has chosen. The choice of aims and values has not been avoided, but simply disguised as something else. And by being disguised as something else, it is removed from scrutiny.

Such a view of educational aims as something which will emerge naturally risks being professionally debilitating, since it suggests that the educator's principal obligations are purely negative ones such as not coercing children, not filling them with knowledge, or not rebuking them for unacceptable behaviour. Taken to its ultimate conclusion, such a view would serve as a justification for educational laissez-faire or even anarchy.

These conclusions are reinforced by a consideration of the misleading analogy between the growth of an organism whose form is predetermined unless development is impeded by adverse circumstances, and the so-called moral or intellectual growth of a person. For this latter process consists of the acquisition of desired forms of behaviour, knowledge and understanding which are not at all predetermined.

An acorn either grows into an oak tree, or it grows into nothing. To some extent this is true of human beings. A baby boy will not grow into a sea-lion or a hippopotomus. No amount of education will affect this issue.

But education may affect whether he becomes a master criminal, a civil rights leader, a concert pianist or a drug pedlar. The acorn precontains the oak, and all you have to do is let it grow. But neither the sperm nor the egg precontains the civil rights leader or the pianist. The one has to be initiated into a tradition of radical dissent

– for political dissent is not just a spontaneous outburst but the product of a long tradition which is learnt, cherished and passed down from one generation to the next. The other has to learn a great deal of music – which is also the product of a social tradition.

Of course, you cannot become a concert pianist or whatever without the necessary 'potential'. But such potential is not specific and determined, like the genetic code in the acorn which establishes the main characteristics of the fully grown oak. Human potential is to be seen, rather, as the absence of inhibiting factors such as mental deficiency, lack of physical stamina, deafness or just plain stumpy fingers. Potentiality of this kind may be fulfilled in a wide variety of human achievements depending on the educational experience the individual encounters or fails to encounter. These will determine whether this child's long sensitive fingers or whatever enable him to grow up into a Horowitz, a Fagin or a Don Juan.

But the growth metaphor is not entirely without value. The gardener may choose what sorts of flowers he wants (i.e. make value judgements, in this case of an aesthetic kind) but beyond a certain limit he cannot force the pace. If he wants good results he has to know a good deal about plants and the conditions under which they flourish. Likewise the educator, once the initial value judgements about ends have been made, needs to know a great deal about how children work. This can sometimes be learnt from psychologists, child developers and other empirical researchers, in much the same way that a gardener might learn something from a botanist or a chemist. From them the gardener may learn how to produce certain flowers, but not which flowers are the most beautiful or look the most appropriate in a particular setting.

Like the slogan urging us to foster the child's natural growth, those telling us to have regard to his interests and needs are admirable in certain important respects but are, once again, deficient as guides for what our specific educational aims should be. Their value lies in the fact that they require us to respect the child and not only to consider how children are at a particular stage in their lives, but also to be sensitive to the way in which they respond to the various educational offerings that are placed before them.

They are also admirable in their attempt to avoid the arbitrary and unthinking imposition of traditional aims which may not always be appropriate to all children. It is certainly possible to imagine and sometimes even find expression of attitudes and assumptions which suggest that teachers should not be too concerned to benefit the child, but see it as their task to turn him into something more useful or simply less troublesome to adults.

In discussing the child's interests it is worthwhile to distinguish briefly between his ethical interests (what is *in* his interest) and his psychological interests (what he is interested *in*). This is often dismissed as a mere banality, and there is certainly little chance of anyone confusing the two. In the present context we are principally concerned with psychological interests as a possible source of aims, for this is how our slogan is usually interpreted. Nevertheless, the assertion that what we do in school and the changes we bring about in the child should be in his interests rather than in the interests of someone else – parents, government, future employers and the like – is not without importance.

This does not mean that children may not be taught things which will enable them to contribute to the well-being of society, or to behave in a morally and socially acceptable way. For others, including adults, also have rights and it is reasonable to suppose that it is not in the child's interest to become a social outcast. An education which enables him to participate in society if he so chooses and to understand the implications if he does not is clearly defensible in these terms, and is to be distinguished from an exploitative schooling in docility and obedience with which it is sometimes confused.

It is commonly argued that a child's psychological interests (what he happens to be interested *in*) provide little indication of what are worthwhile educational ends. In support of this claim it is often tritely said that he may, after all, be interested in all kinds of trivial and undesirable things. Pulling the wings off flies, making mud pies and counting the blades of grass in public parks are commonly cited as examples.

It may be thought that the child would not be disposed to take an interest in these or any other activities unless he had something to learn by so doing. But if these were to be envisaged as educational activities their content would need to be spelt out in terms of the manual skills, facts about the world, underlying concepts and so on that were being learnt, rather than in terms of the activities themselves. The child playing with mud pies would be learning about the experiences brought to him by the sense of touch, muscular control and the manipulation of malleable materials

40

rather than simply how to make mud pies. The educational justification of the activity resides in the value of these learnings rather than in the fact of the child's interest. But, of course, this interest may provide useful pointers as to what he is ready to learn, as well as a valuable means of enabling him to learn it.

Just possibly during the child's earliest years anything and everything may be both interesting and a source of valuable learning. As he gets older, however, it seems clear that some guidance other than contingent fascination with what happens to catch his attention may be required. This is to ensure economy and sequence as well as providing opportunities for pupils to become interested in activities which have educational potential and may later prove absorbing, but at present leave them unmoved or uncomprehending.

Knowledge of what a particular child or children of this age or of a particular social background happen in general to be interested in may be extremely helpful in deciding what means to use (what projects to plan, what tasks to set) in order to teach certain skills or important understandings. In addition, once an acceptable range of educational activities has been identified there are good reasons, both motivational and ethical, for allowing pupils' relatively stable interests to determine choices within that range. The choice between chemistry and pornography may not be an acceptable one (however great the interest of the occasional thirteen-year-old in the latter), but the choice between chemistry and German might well be made on a basis of interest.

If interests are to be guided in order to secure certain educational aims, the interests themselves cannot be the source from which we derive our aims. As with the language of growth, that of interests is important in directing our attention to the child and to the most effective means of promoting his learning. The study of what children are interested in may also furnish important clues as to which aims it is expedient to attempt with particular children at particular times. Ultimately, however, those aims must be derived from other considerations and defended on other grounds. Once again, the language of interests, like that of growth, may distract us from the task of making value judgements about aims, without ultimately enabling us to avoid it.

Discussion of the child's supposed needs may also lead us to assume that decisions of educational policy may ultimately be made on the basis of objectively ascertainable facts. In the modern

41

world, it may be suggested, the child, if he is to flourish, needs numeracy, literacy and, say, a range of vocational skills in much the same way that he needs food, oxygen and shelter. It does, perhaps, also make sense to speak of his having certain psychological needs. No doubt there are things such as stability, affection, self-esteem and security without which the child's life is miserable and without which he is not going to be in any state to learn much at all. Of course, these needs have to be met, if not elsewhere, then at school. But they do not tell us a great deal about the educational ends we ought to be pursuing, even if they draw our attention to the minimal conditions under which they may be achieved.

The question of whether the fact that someone needs something is in itself a good reason for providing it has been much debated. Two facts about the logic of needs have received particular attention. The first of these is that the question of whether or not someone needs something is not an entirely empirical one. To say that someone needs something is usually to say that he needs it in order to do or get something else (Barry, 1965, p. 48; White, 1974), though it is often not necessary to specify what that something else is. A person needs food if he is not to die of starvation, but we do not normally feel it necessary to debate the value judgement that someone ought not to be allowed to starve to death.

But it may also be said that a young man needs to learn to use a jemmy if he is to make a decent living as a burglar and a girl needs to learn to type if she is to become a typist. Whether these needs provide grounds for action will depend on our judgement as to the desirability of someone becoming a burglar or a typist respectively. Many of the alleged needs of pupils are therefore not really *their* needs at all. It is ultimately the typist's employer who needs her typing skills. Similar remarks may be made when it is said that a waiter needs to speak several languages, a chef needs to know how to keep his work station clean, and so on. Consequently, a set of educational aims based on the 'needs', especially the 'vocational needs', of children might turn out to be very far from child-centred indeed.

A second observation that has been made about needs is that, far from enabling us to escape from value judgements, statements about needs may presuppose certain rather precise social and other external standards (Komisar, 1961, p. 25). Obvious cases in point are when we say things like 'that boy needs a bath', 'this pupil needs to give more attention to his handwriting and spelling' and

42

'that young man needs to show more respect when speaking to adults'.

Indeed, if someone attempts to take the pupil's supposed needs as a guide to what the content of education should be, he is in something of a cleft stick. On the one hand he may find himself defending a rather narrowly utilitarian or even vocational sort of education. It might be easy to see, for example, that everyone needs minimal numeracy and literacy and one of a range of vocational skills with some 'generic' breadth built in as a hedge against technological shift. But it is not so easy to justify in these terms any much wider range of educational aspiration. A future professional musician might seem to need a knowledge of music, but it would be difficult to see why anyone else should.

On the other hand, he may attempt to escape from this position by saying that the pupil not only needs a basic educational survival kit, but a full range of other educational and cultural acquisitions 'in order to participate fully in society' or become a 'fully developed human being'. But if he makes this move he may be called upon to say which of society's many activities our pupils ought to be prepared to participate in, and give his reasons for preferring some rather than others. As regards becoming a fully developed human being, this rather brings us back to the problems we found with natural growth. Human beings have potential for developing in many directions and the problem of educational aims is deciding which kinds of development should be fostered and which discouraged.

Chapter Five

The Trouble with Rational Autonomy

Though many educational philosophers find both 'happiness' and the child-centred aims discussed in the previous section unsatisfactory as expressions of educational aims, they may nevertheless attach great importance to the aim of developing what they term the pupil's 'autonomy'. Indeed, it may often seem to be taken as the *raison d'être* of the entire educational enterprise (Crittenden, 1978, p. 105). Peters (1973c) bases an important part of his justification of education on the fact that the sciences and humanities provide information that will enable the individual to answer for himself the question 'What ought I to do?' 'How', that is, 'ought I to live my life?' White (1973, pp. 23–5) selects for his compulsory curriculum activities which, though not in his view in any objective sense intrinsically worthwhile, provide the range of experience necessary if the pupil is to be in a position to choose his own future way of life. Degenhardt (1982, pp. 81–93) gives a similar reason for valuing knowledge and Jonathan (1983, p. 6), criticizing developments in the direction of a more vocationally oriented curriculum, claims that 'the purpose of education is to give the young an understanding of the world and the ability to make considered choices about how to live in it'.

Dearden (1972d, p. 448; 1975, p. 3), among others, has pointed out that autonomy originally referred to the condition of a city or state that was self-governing or free to live under its own laws rather than obeying those imposed upon it by others. In relation to individuals, an autonomous person is one who is free and able to make his own choices and decisions and, ultimately, to determine

44

the course of his own life and personal development. An individual's autonomy may be threatened from two directions. He may be coerced, pressurized or misled by others. Or he may be deflected from his chosen purposes by internal compulsions, irrational desires and sundry other weaknesses of the will.

In an educational context the promotion of someone's autonomy may therefore take place at various levels. At one level, one may set about removing the external constraints upon an individual's life choices and options for educational and personal development. An educational system in which teachers or officials rather than pupils themselves decide which pupils are to learn what subjects would be contrary to the principle of autonomy at this level.

We also promote the autonomy of pupils when we attempt to develop in them the qualities of mind and character which will help and encourage them to make their own choices freely. Clearly, qualities of independence and self-confidence are part of the story. But the making of valid choices also entails possessing both a good deal of information about the world and the options it has to offer and the likely consequences of one's various options.

It also involves a critical attitude to what one is told, for most of what we know and believe comes to us on the say-so of others. Many of the things we do are necessarily done at the behest or suggestion of others or in accordance with their example or established practice. Being critical, however, is not simply an attitude of mind. We cannot properly be critical without both factual knowledge and a grasp of the ways in which various claims are to be criticized, the standards of evidence it is appropriate to expect or the canons of rationality that must be met.

At this point, however, a difficulty enters the argument. It would appear to follow from the foregoing that to choose autonomously is to choose rationally, to do as one does because there are good reasons for so doing. To do otherwise is supposed to be blind 'plumping' for one course rather than another or acting heteronomously as a result of pressure, error or some other form of internal or external compulsion. If, however, one acts in accordance with reason and reason leads ineluctably to certain conclusions, the scope for individual freedom of choice seems somewhat limited. The aim that people should act autonomously, if this means rationally, begins, paradoxically, to look like a subtle form of manipulation. A further twist to the argument may be given by the suggestion that what passes for rationality in a particular society may be influenced or even determined by the interests of certain powerful groups.

This difficulty parallels one that is encountered in the field of social and political philosophy. Among Anglo-Saxon philosophers, especially, there is a common-sense view (Cranston, 1953, p. 40) that freedom simply denotes the absence of constraint. To be free on this view is simply not to be prevented from doing whatever one happens to want to do at a given moment.

Freedom in this negative sense is a useful principle to appeal to in demanding political independence, an innocent person's release from prison or rejection of the oppressive constraints of social respectability. Those who hold this view of freedom suppose that citizens are responsible adults who may be assumed to be capable of understanding the implications and consequences of their actions and ought therefore only to be constrained in order to protect the equal freedom of others.

Critics, however, suggest that such a negative view of freedom is inadequate and argue for a more positive conception according to which the individual is not only free from physical constraint or actual interference but is, in a far fuller sense, in control of his actions. To demonstrate the shortcomings of the negative concept of freedom one might point out that there certainly exist people who suffer from compulsions or addictions. We have also long been aware that it is perfectly possible for someone to wish at one level to follow the good which he sees and approves, while actually doing something less laudable. One may be perfectly conscious of acting against one's better judgement, or against one's will even when no obvious external coercion is being employed.

Someone's immediate wants may be the result of momentary whims, of manipulation or persuasion, hidden or otherwise, or of calculated appeals to emotion or other irrational considerations. They may also be the result of prejudice, ignorance, or just plain failure to think things through. For all it has been abused, it is also difficult not to see some validity in the notion of 'false consciousness' which may lead us to 'choose freely' things we should not choose if we fully understood and considered what was involved.

It will be seen that the notion of positive freedom bears some resemblance to that of autonomy. Although the term rational autonomy is invariably viewed favourably, however, the theory of positive freedom has received something of a bad press. It is often used to refer to the abuses of totalitarian regimes. In the political field, Rousseau (1762a, 4.I, pp. 85–7) must be credited with popularizing the distinction between what people happen to want and their 'real' or rational will. It is unfortunate that he should also have spoken of 'forcing' people to be free in the sense of obliging them to obey their own 'real will' as expressed in laws passed by the majority votes of legislative assemblies. From here it is a short step to the definition of liberty as voluntary submission to some authority of which the writer approves (Peters, 1966, pp. 187–8). Thus, freedom may be thought of as submission to the law of reason or even obedience to the law of the land (Benn and Peters, 1959, p. 213). Christians may speak of God's service as perfect freedom and totalitarian invaders are inclined to speak of 'liberating' the territories they invade, even when their armies are fiercely resisted by the local inhabitants. As with rational autonomy, positive or, as it is sometimes called, 'rational' freedom comes to look uncommonly like slavery.

Yet clearly educators must approve of something resembling the positive concept. If ignorance, prejudice, ideology, uncritically accepted social assumptions and lack of reflection prevent people from doing the things they would wish to do, it is precisely these shortcomings that education is peculiarly suited to combat. Educators characteristically oblige children to do things they do not immediately want to do in the belief that restrictions placed on their negative freedom now will be more than compensated by their enhanced autonomy or positive freedom later on (White, 1973, p. 22), as a result of the useful things they are about to learn.

We are therefore back with our problem of reaching an understanding of the concept of positive, rational freedom or autonomy which will enable educators to aim at liberating individuals from impediments to their rationality and promoting the enhanced freedom that accompanies its exercise, without suggesting that they aim to impose particular beliefs, values and ways of life upon them simply because the educators themselves find them edifying. In attempting to solve this problem it is helpful to give some attention to a related concept also closely concerned with individual freedom, namely that of authenticity.

This latter quality is supposed to represent a thoroughgoing rejection of the values and assumptions that have traditionally given meaning and purpose to people's lives. This rejection arises from the insight, or supposed insight, that such values and assumptions are without foundation. Its most widely known expression is probably Nietzsche's remark that 'God is dead'. That is, since we are no longer able to believe in a personal God the Divine Will can no longer serve as a sufficient reason for acting in a certain way or striving for certain ideals. When it comes to deciding what to do or how to live our lives we are thrown back on our own devices. We are answerable to no one, and there is no one to take the responsibility from us. When Nietzsche speaks of the 'shabby' or disreputable origins of our value assumptions he normally has in mind such supposedly enlightened values as equality, humanity and modesty. Far from being sublime and noble in origin, he claims, these are simply the result of the envious and spiteful desire of the mediocre majority of mankind to drag the few really courageous and effective individuals in the world down to their own level. Other writers, however, have argued with considerable plausibility that the whole range of our values and other basic assumptions are similarly questionable. Many people these days accept that not only the value system of a society, but the whole of its intellectual and cultural life simply reflects and serves to defend the interests of a dominant class. Others hold that the 'Christian' virtues of chastity and family life simply reflect the power relations in a patriarchal society in which women are regarded as property. All of these arguments are of a debunking kind according to which 'everything is something else, but slightly less respectable'. In the arts the notion of authenticity has been immensely productive, both as a literary theme and in the rejection of conventional forms. In life, as in art, authenticity consists in not doing the done thing simply because it is the done thing. Simply to follow convention is to act in bad faith, to pretend that one cannot affect the outcome of events, and to abrogate the responsibility for one's choices. According to more extreme interpretations of the notion of authenticity, not only is social convention an inadequate ground for doing one thing rather than another, but bad faith is entailed in accepting any reason whatsoever as overriding.

The task of the individual facing a moral dilemma is not, by a process of ratiocination, to *discover* what one should do, but to *decide* what to do – not to fathom out one's pre-existing obligations (for there are none) but to 'create one's destiny'. Nor, as Cooper shows (1983, pp. 8–12), will it do either to act in accordance with some conception of one's 'true self' or simply to respond to one's passing whim, for despite the fact that many seekers after authenticity have been tempted to follow one or other of these two courses, both attempt to sidestep the making of a genuinely authentic decision.

Needless to say, anyone who accepts the value of authenticity as described above must take a dim view of an educational programme supposed to be based on 'rational arguments' purporting to show conclusively that some activities are more worthwhile than others. He must take an even dimmer view of the claim that a certain kind of education will make people autonomous by providing them with the rational grounds and procedures for correctly choosing one mode of behaviour or one way of life in preference to others.

Such a rejection underlies much of the radical educational writing which appeared in the 1970s. This includes the work not only of Illich (1971) and the deschoolers but also of such writers as Holt (e.g. 1977) and Bereiter (1973), as well as the proponents of the Free School discussed by Crittenden (1978, pp. 108–16). These writers are concerned to attack not only the coercive aspect of compulsory schooling but all efforts to implement a predetermined set of curricular aims, however 'rationally justifiable' they might seem.

In contrast with the notion of rational autonomy, that of authenticity has often received short shrift from educational philosophers, Cooper (1983) and Bonnett (1986) being notable exceptions. Dearden (1972d, p. 457) dismisses the idea of 'criterionless choices' as a contradiction in terms. Crittenden (1978, pp. 108–16) has drawn attention to the supposedly self-referring nature of extreme demands for authenticity. If all virtues are supposed to be shabby, disreputable and invalid, he argues, it is difficult to see why the virtue of authenticity alone should be worthy of approval. Critics of the notion of authenticity also make much of the opacity of many attempts to characterize it. This, it might be thought, is indication enough of the concept's incoherence. And to be sure Bonnett's 'direct relationship to Being' (1986, p. 123), 'openness to things in themselves' and 'necessary levelled off quality of a principled way of relating to things' (p. 124) do not inspire confidence. Despite the failure of philosophers to give a coherent account of the concept, however, there exist abundant literary creations in which the virtue of authenticity is exemplified and understood by countless ordinary readers and theatre-goers. Sartre's Hugo (in *Les Mains Sales*), Anouilh's Antigone and Bolt's Sir

Thomas More (in *A Man for All Seasons*) may be taken as obvious examples among a multitude. The first of these accepts liquidation by his revolutionary comrades, rather than have it be that his act of political assassination was simply the result of a jealous impulse. The second allows herself to be immured alive for refusing to leave her brother's body unburied as political expediency demands, and the third goes to the scaffold rather than concur in Henry VIII's marriage to Anne Boleyn. These characters are shown to act as they do despite rational prudence, common sense and even humanity towards those around them. On any rational criterion they would act otherwise than they do. Yet the audience assents to the course of action they choose.

Significantly, the response evoked by these three 'authentic' characters is not moral approval – all may in fact be criticized on moral grounds – but admiration. To have acted otherwise would certainly not have been morally wrong, but slightly contemptible, disappointing. Something valuable would have been lost. But, of course, they do not act as they do *in order* to be admired. That would be an act of exquisite bad faith.

They do not invoke any kind of principle to justify their action and such reasons as they do give would not withstand, and are not supposed to withstand, any kind of further examination. To speak of their choosing to act as they do for the reasons they give as making 'criterionless choices', as if it were somehow ultimately possible to do otherwise, however, rests on a drastically oversimplified view of the world of values and value judgements.

It would certainly be a fine thing if the whole field of human actions were matched by a set of reasons for and against, each with its own tariff of desirability or undesirability. One might, perhaps, imagine a form of moral pyramid in which, when the reasons for alternative courses of action seemed evenly balanced, one could refer to some form of 'higher criterion' and beyond that to some form of supreme good. If the moral world were thus tidily arranged, choice would indeed be a matter of patient ratiocination until the right solution was found. In such a world there need be no anguish, no disagreement or moral conflict between rational people, and certainly no tragedy.

Would that the world were thus simple, but it is not. Within particular institutions or particular activities there may be clear and obvious grounds for choosing one course of action rather than another. A businessman faced with a choice of investing at 10 per cent or at 12 per cent, given the same risks, is not short of a criterion upon which to base his decision. The same is true for a military commander faced with the choice of risking the loss of a small squad or a whole company, so long as all the men in both squad and company are equally anonymous to him. But supposing the small squad contains the son of a close friend? Professionally speaking – that is, *qua* military commander – his situation is unchanged. The criterion of decision remains the size of the military loss to be incurred. No doubt many individuals placed in this position would resolve the dilemma by steadfastly refusing to look beyond the bounds of the professional role. But that is precisely what bad faith consists in; an attempt to define the situation in such a way that only certain criteria of conduct can be considered and certain reasons for action are ruled out.

The commander says 'I am a soldier therefore I have no option but to sacrifice the squad.' But he could say 'I am this man's friend. How can I allow his son to be killed when I could prevent it?' In the end he must either allow himself to be a soldier who neglects his duty for the sake of personal friendship, or a friend who neglects friendship for the sake of his military duty. Two important and long-standing values which have hitherto guided his actions and provided him with his conception of his own identity are in conflict, and one of them must be given up. He quite literally creates his own future since, from now on, he must see himself as one or other of the two kinds of person mentioned above. There is no unchallengeable criterion which will enable him to choose one rather than the other.

Some critical readers will deny this, saying, for example, that he must clearly do his military duty, given the chaotic consequences if everyone put personal considerations first. ('Armies just could not function on that basis, etc.') But others, equally critical, might just as well argue that there would be little point in winning battles if friendship counted for so little.

It will be seen that, as the argument progresses, more and more general principles are invoked and we become further and further removed from the actual issue the individual has to resolve. If this is continued for too long in the presence of a serious decision in the real world, the discussion risks appearing not increasingly pro-found but frivolous. The individual must decide one way or the other. Not all countervailing considerations can be defeated. If all decision is not to be paralysed some, though perfectly valid, must simply be ignored. Guilt, not just irrational feelings of guilt, but real guilt for the values betrayed, may be incurred, and must be borne.

The above is no doubt a rather dramatic example of a moral dilemma, which is certainly somewhat removed from the classroom. Nevertheless, some decisions pupils have to make about their educational careers may have this quality of defining the future rather than flowing naturally from a weighing of the alternatives according to a single pre-established criterion.

Choices of subjects and courses may well determine what a person will become. The attractions of a rewarding vocational course and the prospect of comfortable employment now versus the rigors and satisfactions of an extended period of study in a non-vocational discipline are incommensurable, and the relative advantages of each are incalculable.

The main purpose of the illustration, however, was to make a rather different point about the nature of human choices. Those advocates of rational autonomy who speak dismissively about the mindless plumping implied by the notion of a criterionless option appear to assume that, when it comes to making serious choices, there are only two possibilities:

(1) To act in a certain way and not otherwise as the result of a faultless chain of reasoning linking back to some equally rational and objectively identified criterion or principle.
(2) The blind, irresponsible pursuit of whim, caprice or hazard.

Yet clearly these two possibilities do not exhaust the field. If it is accepted that criterionless options of the kind I have tried to illustrate sometimes exist, readers will also be aware that such choices are often made in a spirit that is far from one of irresponsible plumping or caprice. Such decisions are often a matter of agonizing reflection and discussion and the most rigorous and exhaustive process of contemplating and following through the implications of the various alternatives available.

It is also, perhaps, of some significance that at the end of such a process, the agent will often emerge with a clear and confident conviction as to what course of action he should follow and have become a person of greater stature and understanding than before. The misunderstandings which surround this issue appear to arise from a failure to make two important distinctions.

The first of these is between having reasons for action, for doing

this and not that, and having (or attempting to discover) some
overriding criterion which clinches the matter and rules all
contrary considerations out of court. To deny the possibility of the
second is not to deny the importance and validity of the first.
Though our military commander was not justified in turning to
either the principle of military duty or that of friendship to resolve
his dilemma without further ado, he would have been entirely right
to pass all the relevant considerations seriously under review.
These would include the importance of impartiality and military
discipline and his own insistence on these things in the past, his
affection for his friend and his friend's son, the ties of gratitude and
mutual obligation that bind the two families and so on. Good faith
and responsible decision require that all of these matters weigh
with him though none finally clinches the matter. He may debate
with real or imaginary confidants, but in the end he must decide
and, like the judge in Camus's *La Peste*, no one can help him.

The second distinction to be made is between reasons which
must supposedly be persuasive upon all rational beings and
reasons which will be persuasive upon a particular individual,
given his particular talents, inclinations, obligations, past history
and so on. To suppose that all reasons are of the first kind is to fail to
recognize the ultimately subjective element present in the agent's
decisions about his personal life. To refer to the hackneyed
Sartrean example, someone of one temperament could not be
expected to stay at home to look after his widowed mother when a
war of national liberation is taking place, whereas another could
quite easily do so – though both, if they were not to be guilty of bad
faith, might suffer some moments of doubtful anxiety before
reaching a decision. If an individual were seriously drawn by a life
of adventure and action it is scarcely to be expected that he would
be deterred from taking the opportunity to join an expedition to
explore the Amazon by certain arguments like those of Peters
(1966, ch. 5) to the effect that the most worthwhile activities are
those of an intellectual and cognitive nature. Even if he were
unable to detect any fallacy in the argument in question, it still
would not constitute – and here I employ an expression which
some may find objectionable – a good reason *for him*.

It is tempting to dismiss this subjective element in our choices
and decisions as 'capricious', 'emotional' or in some other way
'irrational'. Alternatively, we may attempt to accommodate it by
saying that someone's own temperament and inclinations consti-

tute one of the elements to be taken into account when rational decisions are made. Both of these moves, however, are invalid. As we have seen, the claim that 'such is my nature' no more provides a final criterion of decision than anything else, while the irreducibly subjective part of an individual is not moved only by whims, but may be swayed by reasons easily recognized as such, but which are not binding upon action in an absolute or conclusive way.

In this chapter we have been concerned with two conceptions of human freedom. At the outset both seemed less than satisfactory. On the one hand, the aim of promoting someone's 'rational autonomy' seemed potentially coercive. On the other, 'authenticity', in so far as it could be understood at all, seemed rootless and capricious, downgrading the part to be played in human conduct by reason and intelligence. As our argument has proceeded we have endeavoured to show that, properly understood, there are not two antithetical and mutually exclusive values involved here, but rather two aspects of a single aspiration. Failure to recognize this fact arises from an unduly simplistic view of the world of values and choices in which human life is carried on.

If this quality of autonomy/authenticity is to be an aim of education, knowledge of the material and human world and of values must be relevant to the choices we have to make. So also must the valid processes and procedures of criticism appropriate to claims and arguments of various kinds. But if it is not to resemble a subtle way of achieving universal conformity, then, after all possible true statements have been made and all valid arguments put, there must remain a certain irreducible indeterminacy in the way an individual may reasonably act. No novel interpretation of moral reasoning is required for this to be possible. Philosophers have long been aware that though moral judgements are by no means entirely subjective, absolute precision in their regard is not possible. Our aim is closer to Arnold's hellenism (Arnold, 1869, ch. 1), in which reason plays freely around many considerations, rather than that hebraism which prescribes the pursuit of 'one thing needful' in the light of one doctrine, however true and irrefutable.

Chapter Six

Children into Workers

Teachers have been criticized (Callaghan, 1976) because their ex-pupils are not up to the job of work that is demanded of them. Parents expect that the education their children receive will enable them to obtain a good job when they leave school and employers expect that the 'products' of our schools will possess the skills and attitudes that will help them run their businesses profitably.

Numerous documents from government, Her Majesty's Inspectors, the Manpower Services Commission and various employers' organizations have all but established the truism that transforming children into workers is the principle justification for our national 'investment' in education. Reference to other aims is relegated to the level of a public relations exercise (Bailey, 1984, pp. 170–2) and such concessions have become increasingly perfunctory.

As was suggested earlier (pp. 22), analysis of the concepts of 'education' and 'training' will not itself enable us to answer the substantive question of whether a major aim of our schools should be to turn children into better workers. It may, nevertheless, be helpful to distinguish training as learning and practice aimed at securing the efficient performance of a particular skill or occupation or the reliable and efficient achievement of particular ends. Training may, of course, involve a substantial cognitive element as well as manual skills. This, however, will be oriented towards the competent performance of the task or occupation for which the individual is being trained, rather than aimed at promoting more general insights into the nature of the world and human life. In addition to knowledge and skills, training may also involve the schooling of certain attitudes and responses to the point where they become automatic. Use of the term 'training' implies no moral judgement, negative or positive, about the activities or ends for which the individual is being trained. Assassins and terrorists may be trained, as well as musicians and accountants. Prima facie the acquisition of useful skills would seem to be desirable, provided this does not compromise other values or entail the loss of other opportunities.

In the light of these remarks, various positions are possible regarding the part which ought to be played in the upbringing of children by training and preparation for the work they will do in later life.

Elitism:
the Separation of Education and Work

At one extreme we may consider a traditional elitist conception of education in which preparation for work played little part, for the simple reason that work itself was expected to play little significant part in the future lives of the pupils concerned. In so far as education was a preparation for life, it was for a life of cultured leisure. If these pupils were to fulfil a particular social function it was that of government, or the direction of important affairs. This would be at several removes from reality rather than at the level of detailed management, not to mention manual operation.

Presumably no one, even in the most privileged schools, continues to think that their pupils are destined for a life consisting entirely of leisure (except perhaps in the sick sense of leisure to mean unemployment, which is not really leisure at all). The distinction, however, continues to be made between vocational education, which is a preparation for work, and a 'liberal' education which is in some other sense a preparation for life, or a preparation for those aspects of life which are not work. The term 'liberal education' contains an ambiguity which has been helpful in making it acceptable in the conditions of the modern world. On the one hand it has been seen as an education suitable for a 'free man', that is, someone who is not obliged to earn his living by bondage to a particular employer. More recently, however, the emphasis has been on the freeing or liberalizing effects of such an education which frees the individual from the narrow perspective of what Bailey (1984) calls 'the present and the particular' and supports his status as a chooser of his own values and way of life.

Vocation as a Motivator

Even this interpretation of a liberal education may seem outmoded and inappropriate to most of the pupils currently in our schools. With its continuing historical and literary element it too may be criticized as elitist and suitable only to a leisured class. The task of choosing those activities that are most worthwhile would, after all, seem to be mainly of interest to those whose economic needs are already taken care of and whose main problem in life is discovering the best use to make of their time.

Much of the content of what has, until recently, been regarded as a typical liberal education was in itself of considerable vocational relevance. This was not merely for a leisured class whose 'vocation was to enjoy' (Dewey, 1916, p. 312) but for lawyers and clerics for whom knowledge of ancient languages and the habits of textual quotation were essential professional skills. Continued study of these things may simply represent a failure to adapt to changing times, like a tribe that continues to teach the techniques of a sabre-tooth tiger scaring long after such creatures have become extinct and been replaced by marauding bears (Benjamin, 1939).

Concentration on the study of dead languages and literary classics is certainly vulnerable to this criticism. It is also true that watered down versions of this curriculum that found their way into secondary modern and even grammar schools did little to promote rationality or disinterested commitment to intrinsically worthwhile activities. Even in successful grammar schools Latin verbs, lyric poetry and Shakespearian tragedies were simply 'swotted up' in order to get into the most prestigious universities with a view to graduating into the most lucrative jobs. In less successful schools the content of a so-called 'middle-class education' was often unintelligible to pupils and teachers alike, and left both untouched.

In the light of these criticisms progressive educators in the present century have canvassed the view that, in order to meet the practicalities of the modern world and engage the interests of the majority of pupils, education should become more pragmatic and problem solving (Kilpatrick, 1951, pp. 248–62) and shorn of inert ideas (Whitehead, 1929). In the case of some children at least, education should aim to be 'practical' and 'realistic' (Ministry of Education, 1963, p. 32).

It is important, however, that we should carefully distinguish the aims of this movement from current demands that schools should

turn out pupils more precisely adapted to the workshop requirements of employers. Both official publications and supporters of
the modern notion of 'Education for Capability' (Burgess, 1986)
make use of the rhetoric of earlier progressives in criticizing a
liberal education based on knowledge and understanding rather
than action (Bailey, 1984, pp. 187–8). Earlier writers (see e.g.
Vaizey, 1962) were also inclined to refer to the economic ill effects
of what they regarded as an outmoded form of education, and were
prepared to see up-to-date (including vocational) interests as a way
into the education of young people who were left untouched by
what was currently on offer. But their overriding concern remained the individual-centred and morally unimpeachable one of
bringing pupils to an understanding of themselves and the world
about them. In the words of Dewey (1916, p. 309) the aim was not
education *for* but *through* practical occupations. Vocational relevance therefore became 'an organising principle for information
and ideas; for knowledge and intellectual growth'. Such an
education would, Dewey hoped, provide not only the motivation to
reach out for relevant information but also the reason to retain it.
The essential aim was 'not that of making schools an adjunct to
manufacture and commerce, but of utilising the factors of industry
to make school life more active, more connected with out of school
experience' (p. 316). Dewey clearly distinguishes between the
conception of vocational education and what he terms 'trade
education' as a means of securing technical efficiency in special-
ized future pursuits. With great prescience he anticipates the
danger that education of this latter sort would perpetuate social
divisions in 'a hardened form' and 'taking its stand upon the feudal
dogma of social predestination, would assume that some are to
continue to be wage earners under economic conditions like the
present' (p. 316).

Schooling for Docility

For the so-called 'deschoolers' and other educational radicals
(Illich, 1971; Bowles and Gintis, 1976; Althusser, 1972; see also
Wringe, 1984, pp. 33–42) what goes on in schools and similar
institutions is all too obviously about the preparation for working
life, though not in the naive way in which this idea is commonly
understood. To such writers the notion of a liberal education

preparing people for a life of autonomous choice seems laughable, for most people have no such choice. Equally suspect is the view that education is concerned with equipping pupils with technical skills and qualifications which will make them more productive employees and more economically successful themselves. On the contrary, they see the effect of schooling as creating not competence and capability but failure and demoralization. Standards and teaching methods in the more prestigious and difficult subjects like mathematics, physics and foreign languages are such that most pupils will make little progress and learn little of any value. Their relative failure will serve to legitimate the status quo and existing inequalities by convincing the majority that they are just not good enough for anything but menial occupations.

Clearly this is an extreme view, for people do learn many things in school that are of value to them, both intrinsically and in more instrumental terms. There are, however, two aspects of schooling that lend support to the radical claim.

First, much that is learned in school is, in fact, not used and may well be forgotten, even in subjects that may have some bearing on the pupil's future occupation. It is notorious that even future technicians use little of the mathematics and science they learnt at school once the relevant examination for their chosen occupation has been taken. The other aspect, which is of more immediate concern in relation to our present subject, is the fact that schemes of vocational education place much emphasis not on certificated or saleable skills and competences but upon such personal and social characteristics as grooming, punctuality and co-operativeness (sometimes decoded as docility). These may make pupils more desirable and manageable employees, but do little to improve their bargaining position in the market place. They remain essentially unskilled workers, even if they are now more acceptable to employers.

The nature of technical advance is such that though a minority of highly skilled technologists may be required, the majority of occupations are consistently de-skilled by the increasing sophistication of machinery and the progressive subdivision of the production process. What industry actually requires, therefore, is not an increasingly skilled workforce, but one that is increasingly flexible and tolerant of boring and tedious activities. Hence the emphasis on the 'moral' qualities of character and flexibility in those that are to alternate between the lowest rungs of the

59

occupational ladder and the dole queue, until permanent unemployment overtakes them in middle life.

Work as an Element in the Good Life

A contrast to this view is that put forward by Mary Warnock (1977, pp. 143–51) to the effect that preparation for work is a perfectly proper part of one's education, since work itself is part of the good life. The good life, Warnock explains, is compounded of three elements: virtue, work and imagination (p. 129). Unfortunately the arguments put forward to justify the inclusion of work are thin, to say the least. Partly they depend on a palpable ambiguity in the meaning of the term 'work' which will be explored below. Apart from this they are that the worker resembles the Nietzschean superman imposing his will (his employer's will, this must mean) on the world (p. 145) and that it is better to support oneself by one's own efforts than to depend on the charity of others (p. 144).

Producing Better Workers

To these four views of the relationship that exists or ought to exist between education and preparation for work we must add a fifth, which we may call the current orthodoxy. This is that education just is, and is quite properly to be seen as, a preparation for adult working life and that as teachers our overriding aim ought to be to ensure that, as future workers, our pupils will be as economically productive and as diligently committed to the work ethic as possible.

Any consideration of what ought to be the relationship between education and the preparation of pupils for work depends on the answers to some prior questions. These concern the moral status of work, the organization of work in our society and the relative values of economic affluence and certain other potentially desirable conditions such as the simple life.

Warnock, as we have seen, holds that work – she says any kind of work – is a necessary part of the good life, and that preparation for work is therefore part of education, properly so called. For human beings, she declares, work – presumably any kind of work – is necessary to their self-fulfilment.

Now, undoubtedly some activities which are described as work are worthwhile and fulfilling in one way or another. When artists, philanthropists, political idealists, reformers and others speak of their work they often refer to a self-chosen activity which they see as worthwhile, either intrinsically or because of the end it is supposed to achieve. No doubt, many relatively mundane jobs can also be challenging and varied and involve standards of logic, efficiency, integrity, judgement and so on. Many trades, crafts and quite subordinate occupations may be such that each situation provides its own challenges and problems to be met within the standards of a particular craft or the parameters of a particular role.

Work of these kinds presents little difficulty for the claim that it may form part of a version of the good life, and that some kinds of preparation for doing it may be educational. But this can scarcely blind us to the fact that much work is not of this kind at all. Much work is tedious and repetitive, offering no opportunity for the exercise of skill, variation or personal style. It may be concerned with the mass production of objects of no social or aesthetic value, or even of objects which are socially harmful. Many jobs in the tobacco, confectionery and armaments industries must fall into this category. Only extrinsic reasons can be imagined for doing them. One needs the money, or is glad of the chance to be out of the house. It is this kind of work whose moral status must be judged if we are to assess the recommendation that the young should invest time and effort in preparing for it.

Those who perform such work may endure long and exhausting hours, so that waking life is a continuous round of toil, possibly in foul and disagreeable conditions. It is also a salient feature of the situation that in the Western world most work, especially in the manufacturing industry, is not done for the benefit of the individual himself or even of his community, but for the benefit of other private individuals whose profits will enable them to gain for themselves a greater share of this world's goods, for which we are all in competition.

This, of course, is more than obvious. But it is of moral significance that in replacing a liberal education aimed at increasing children's knowledge, understanding and autonomy by a training in skills and pro attitudes to work, our achievement is principally to increase instrumental usefulness of some children to the purposes of others. To this extent children are being viewed as

61

a resource to be developed rather than as potential agents in their own right.

Undoubtedly, there will be some who will say that we ought not to be hypersensitive on this point, and will remind us that value judgements are notoriously subject to variation from time to time. Those who seek a return to more Victorian values than our own will certainly argue that it is to the advantage of the child to be able to find employment in later life, and that if a more work-oriented curriculum enables more people to do this, so much the better. Against this, however, it may be asked whether the provision of more vocational education does not simply sharpen the competition for a relatively fixed number of jobs.

To provide more people with certain skills is to render those skills more plentiful and, by the law of supply and demand, to drive down the price which their possessors may demand for them in the market place. Ultimately, our response to this question must depend on whether we think the number of people employed or unemployed depends on the skills they possess, or upon structural factors such as the financial policies of governments.

Someone who felt that a society in which enterprises run for private profit was an overriding evil would find it difficult to approve an educational practice which bolstered the system by making the worker more efficient or co-operative. Such a person would necessarily regard it as a priority to work for a political order in which enterprises benefited either the community as a whole or, perhaps, a co-operative of their workers.

Those concerned with the moral status of work might also be troubled by the thought that happiness and the good life were to be found in the return to a simpler mode of existence rather than in affluence and an abundance of the things that toil currently serves to produce. Doubtless this view has much to recommend it. As noted above, many manufactured items may have neither aesthetic nor social worth. Labour in the pursuit of affluence may be carried to excess, so that it displaces other aspirations in the individual. It may be counter-productive in squandering resources, and destructive of the environment upon which some aspects of the good life may depend.

Nevertheless, it is a contingent fact about human beings that work – someone's work – is actually necessary to produce what we need to survive. It is also hard to deny that, for many, life is nearer the good life because of the various means of transport, communication, health, study and even comfort and convenience which work produces. Since all depend for survival and an acceptable way of life on the products of toil it may seem that in an ideal world – in which toil were nevertheless a necessity – all should bear their part of it. Barring incapacity there seems manifest justice in the dictum that those who will not work should not benefit from the work of others. If training is necessary before anyone can work in a socially efficient way, then it seems quite legitimate to require all to undergo such training, if they propose to eat.

Furthermore, since toil or starve is an option which the human race as a whole cannot baulk, it may also be the case that some experience of toil should play a part in everyone's education if all are truly to understand the nature of such work and the part it plays in human existence.

Regular, serious toil cannot itself be a necessary part of the good life, however, for those who have more intrinsically satisfying ways of earning a living appear to get along very well without it. At best it would seem a necessary evil, for time spent in toil could be spent in more intrinsically worthwhile pursuits, including more satisfying forms of work. But if toil is not itself a necessary part of a satisfying life, the facts of human existence are such that preparedness to undertake it may be regarded as a necessary part of a life that is just. It would also seem to follow that, if certain kinds of work are a necessary evil rather than themselves part of the good life, the lives of those engaged in such work must contain something else. Artists, philanthropists and reformers may live for their work. For many others, by contrast, the promise of fulfilment through labour is fraudulent. It may be that all must work to live, but it would be unacceptable if some were to live, or be taught to live, only to work.

If toil is a necessary evil, training which enables it to be completed more efficiently and reduces the amount of time to be spent on it, or enables it to be replaced by a more challenging or worthwhile form of work seems morally desirable.

To train someone to work more efficiently is therefore not of itself necessarily to lend one's support to an evil state of affairs. This, however, is not to say that such training should be substituted for a significant part of children's education or even that it should play an important part in the life of educational institutions. Among the many caveats to be observed is the possibility that more important educational aims may be impaired. This may occur both because of the diversion of resources, especially the resource of pupil time, and more particularly because of the inherent nature and emphases of training which is directed towards the speedy and efficacious performance of limited instrumental tasks. It is essential to stress this point and spell out our reservations in some detail as these are all too easily shouted down as weak-kneed academic scruples or 'value judgements' which have to give way to the 'hard facts' of economic life.

It is not difficult to identify values with which the emphasis on turning pupils into better workers may seem to be in conflict. These include the traditional aims of teachers to promote pupils' personal development and autonomy by extending their knowledge and imaginative horizons and, above all, the level of their aspirations. They also include such values as rational inquiry and the commitment to non-instrumental goals which liberate the individual from the rat-race of utility and dependence on the approval of authority. The introduction of training at a fairly early stage in the secondary curriculum may also inhibit social mobility and run counter to the principle of equality of opportunity which for many teachers remain important aims. We should not be over-awed by a style of rhetoric which concedes that these aims are no doubt very fine, but points out that if we do not compete successfully with the Japanese or whomever, none of these things will be possible anyway. Most of our educational aims are compatible with a lower level of economic affluence. Marginal increases in industrial efficiency will not affect the long-term destiny of our society and do not justify the sacrifice of major cultural goals or important areas of individual autonomy.

To orient people towards specific occupations – or rather for specific occupational *levels* – before they are fully formed implies acceptance of Dewey's 'mediaeval doctrine of social predestination' referred to earlier. The process of training is necessarily an arduous one, implying a degree of single-minded commitment to the acquisition of certain fairly specific skills. We may compare the part played by, say, pottery classes as a component in someone's general education with the process by which future operatives in the pottery industry are trained. In the first case the intention may be to enable the student to develop a degree of aesthetic judgement in matters of colour, form and proportion, and to enjoy the experience of creating a usable or pleasing artefact by his own efforts. Some such experience is necessary if the individual is to be in a position to choose whether or not such activity is to be a significant element in his own way of life. A degree of discussion, experimentation and freely chosen activity is, of course, in place as well as the disciplines imposed by the craft and its materials. If, at the end of the day, the student comes to value the work of others in this field, but concludes that this activity is not for him, nothing is lost and some unrealistic aspirations may have been laid to rest.

The way in which future operatives are handled is likely to be somewhat different. The processes to be learnt may have little to do with allowing the individual to explore his aesthetic experience or follow his own bent. They will be closely defined by the current practices of the industry and be determined by considerations of economy and managerial control. The trainee who, out of curiosity, expresses an interest in making pots by, say, certain more primitive processes just to see how it works out is likely to experience the rough side of his instructor's tongue. The aim is that he should learn to perform certain tasks as efficiently and reliably as possible. Speculation as to whether it is worth doing or whether something else might be done instead are strictly out of place.

Whereas education may, among other things, provide the experience on which to base one's life choices, to undertake a particular form of training implies that these choices have already been made. One is to work in the pottery factory and must get down to the hard graft of acquiring the necessary knacks and skills and performing them at an appropriate pace. To decide subsequently not to become a potter would imply a certain failure.

To undertake the arduous business of acquiring the skills of even a relatively humble occupation for the instrumental purposes of making a living is to have made a substantial investment of time and effort in the status quo which it may later be difficult to jettison. In terms of one's identity one has 'become' a potter or whatever. When the need for potters disappears, it may not be psychologically easy to write off one's earlier efforts and seek a job of a different kind. One simply becomes an unemployed potter, waiting for the upturn in the economy. Potters are taken as an example at random. Unemployed miners, not to mention redundant teachers and other academics, have proved equally reluctant to abandon their former identity and seek employment other than that for which they have been trained.

Of course, we must all make a choice of occupation and undertake the necessary training in the end. But as such a choice

65

may be hard to change it needs to be delayed for as long as possible and genuinely made by the individual in the light of necessary knowledge and reflection.

The commitment which results from training for a particular occupation has implications not only for the individual but for the social structure as a whole. To have spent much time and effort on one's training is to have acquired a commitment to a continuance of the existing occupational structure as well as to one's own position in it.

Premature vocational education may also contribute to a perpetuation of the existing social order in even more obvious ways. Time spent on vocationally useful learning, even when this is fairly generally applicable at a certain level of employment, is time taken away from learning of other kinds. No prisoner is so effectively imprisoned as one who does not even know of the existence of a world outside his prison, or is led to think that what it contains is 'boring' or 'snobbish' or irrelevant to anything of practical importance. Take children out of their 'useless', 'academic', 'ivory tower' classes in foreign languages, history, Euclidean geometry, English literature or whatever and send them out on work experience into a factory or restaurant or supermarket and you do not increase the chances that they will become judges, archbishops, merchant bankers, or even leading figures in major commercial enterprises.

Of course, they will learn many useful skills – useful, that is, not so much to themselves but to those who *do* become judges, bankers and leading figures in commercial enterprises. For it is certainly useful to such persons that *others* should learn such things as the care of machinery and equipment, keeping one's work station clean and tidy, reporting faults promptly, relating appropriately to workmates and supervisors and so on (Manpower Services Commission, undated). If these skills were truly useful to their possessors, rather than to those who employ their possessors, we should expect parents who pay for their children's education to insist that their children should be the first to acquire them.

The possession of certain useful skills may improve one's position in the employment market and give one a competitive edge over other applicants when it comes to getting one's foot on the lowest rung of the employment ladder. But time spent in having one's nose rubbed in these learnings and commitment to their usefulness alone, and the relative uselessness of other learnings and aspirations may prevent the individual getting much further in life. Indeed, the resultant limitation of views and attitudes will usually render the individual unacceptable as an applicant for more elevated and responsible forms of employment.

In order to defend technical and vocational education against the charge of being limiting or even disabling in an age of rapid technological change, much has been made of the notion of 'generic' skills which, though vocationally relevant, are supposed not to be specific to any one occupation. Strong doubts have been expressed (Bailey, 1984, p. 184; Jonathan, 1983, p. 8) as to whether the notion of a generic skill is a coherent one. More to the point in the present context is the fact that many of the skills held to be generic (keeping one's work station clean, relating appropriately to supervisors, counting singly or in batches) though common to a number of different occupations are highly specific to a particular *level* of employment, namely the lowest, and for this reason may act as a barrier to pupils' mobility or the adoption of more elevated ambitions.

It is undeniable that the economically most successful people in our society spent their youth not in acquiring limited vocational skills but a good, general educational background. Consequently, there is an obvious social danger of vocational education coming to be seen as appropriate to the mass of the future working population while members of the future elite continue to receive, in the private system, a liberal education which is both personally and economically more valuable.

Not only may the conditions and objectives of training subvert the aims of pupil autonomy and social justice. They may also inhibit the aim of promoting rational inquiry and conflict with the teacher's commitment to truth. To questions about the nature of materials being worked on, or the underlying reasons for its behaviour, the trainer is bound to answer: 'Never mind about that, lad, just keep your hand steady and your eye on the machine.' Whereas the educator would welcome his pupil's questions as an opportunity to provide an extended explanation, the trainer would only feel justified in so doing if it were likely to affect the trainee's performance on the job.

There is another aspect to this conflict. Importance has been attached to ensuring that more, and especially abler pupils undertake a career in industry. Clearly, if it is the case that many pupils take up other occupations because they are simply uninformed about industry, or because they are taken in by the gentlemanly ideology that trade is unworthy, then it is a highly desirable part of the educational process to correct this false understanding. What must at least be considered as a possibility, however, is that those in a position to choose have perfectly valid reasons for electing to follow the careers they do. These may be connected with the uncongenial nature of industrial work, material insecurity or the difficulties of reconciling success in industry with an acceptable family and personal life. They may also be of a more idealistic kind, finding public service or the liberal professions more attractive than the pursuit of profit, either for onself or for one's employers.

Careers education is obviously highly desirable if it is what it claims to be: careers *education*, the skilled, professional activity of seeking and passing on to one's pupils accurate, comprehensive information, duly evaluated and interpreted for their benefit. Clearly, however, it would be both educationally and morally unacceptable for schools to 'sell' industry to their pupils, or present it in a falsely attractive light.

'Knowing more about' industry fairly clearly is a proper educational aim. This can be accepted even by the radical who believes the present exploitive relationship between capital and labour to be possible only because the true nature of the situation is concealed from the masses. Knowledge of how industry works is knowledge of the human and social world, of other minds, of other people's lives and experience. It is part of the individual's understanding of the world and his relationship to it, for someone who does not understand the extent to which he or she is materially supported by manufacture is in error about his or her situation. Whatever we may think about the way industry is run, many productive processes are examples of human achievement and ingenuity and many productive enterprises manifestly embody standards of efficiency, economy, prudence, imagination and management of the rules of cause and effect. There are therefore grounds for arguing that a disinterested study of the manufacturing industry forms a proper part of the individual's education in the modern world.

As a corollary to this, however, if study of the world of work is an essential part of the child's education, it must be carried out, not with amateurish good will and enthusiasm, but to proper professional and educational standards as regards the selection of material, economy of presentation and academic regard for accuracy, integrity and truthfulness. A series of talks on the importance and benevolence of industry by representatives of the local chamber of commerce will not meet the bill. Nor will any discussion of the nature of industry or 'the process by which wealth is created' which is constrained to steer clear of political or controversial topics (Bailey, 1984, p. 174).

Finally there are ways in which increased stress on the importance of work may be in conflict with the thoroughly legitimate educational aim of promoting the pupil's happiness and that of others. Workoholism is destructive of family life and both men and women are currently inclined to see only vocational activity as truly fulfilling. Much of the anxiety and stress and many of the identity crises connected with unemployment might be avoided if our education did more to encourage us to see work and the material benefits it brings as but one part of our life among others.

In circumstances in which most school leavers will not find employment and many adults will experience extended periods of unemployment it might be thought that education would prepare individuals for this situation by de-emphasizing the importance of work, and by stressing the value of leisure, family relationships, recreational and voluntary activity and even the pleasures of the simple life. This, however, would be to fail to appreciate important functional aspects of both education and unemployment – or rather the threat of unemployment. The effectiveness of this threat as a means of discipline in the workplace and elsewhere would be gravely compromised if a generation of young people were to come to believe that there might be better things to do with one's life anyway than to spend it working, or that there were more satisfying if less financially rewarding forms of work than employment as it is usually understood.

The essential truth expressed by the metaphors of wage-slavery, the treadmill and the rat-race is that finding value in things other than material advantage is bound to be liberating. However hard and efficiently we work, the instrumental benefits of our efforts may depend not on our own dedication and skill but on the approval of authority or on the good will of those who control the conditions of our work. And this approval, these conditions, may often be withheld at will. The more committed we are to our work, the more we have invested in learning to work efficiently for the reward and approval of others, the greater is our enslavement.

PART III

Aims and Society

Chapter Seven

Supporting Law and Order

It is expected of schools that they will make a contribution to the harmonious and orderly functioning of society. They are often blamed for the prevalence of crime, violence and civil disorder, and the incidence of delinquency among pupils has been taken as a measure of a school's effectiveness (Rutter, 1979, pp. 110–13).

In considering whether, and in what ways, the support of law and order is an appropriate educational aim one must begin by noting that it is perfectly proper for a society to adopt measures to protect itself, its institutions, its citizens and their way of life and property. This is subject to the proviso that the society in question is a reasonably just one. Needless to say, the question of whether a particular society is 'reasonably just' is necessarily contentious. It is hoped that the following two chapters will provide for some reflection on what are to count as morally acceptable social and political arrangements. In the meantime this deliberately vague expression is used to avoid two opposite implications, neither of which are intended.

On the one hand, it is not intended to justify conformity to the arbitrary demands of just any regime, however tyrannical. In an obviously unjust society the forces of 'law and order' and those in the education system who see it as their aim to support them must often be regarded simply as the agents of oppression.

But equally it is not intended to imply that a society must be absolutely and perfectly just before it is legitimate to give one's support to good order and the normal decencies of everyday life. Even in a society that contained a fair measure of systematic injustice, it might still be right to bring up young people to refrain

73

from indscriminate violence, vandalism, theft, fraud, and other anti-social acts.

The out-and-out revolutionary will reject any such compromise, arguing that this merely helps to cement an unjust status quo. On this view, people should be encouraged to do all they can to undermine public morale and disrupt public order so as to hasten the collapse of society and allow the building of utopia to begin. It is, however, by no means obvious that such a cataclysm will always lead to an improved state of affairs or that – criticisms of 'gradualism' notwithstanding – improvement may not be brought about in at least some societies without any such event. Even in a revolutionary situation, furthermore, one might wish those who are to take part in the revolution to distinguish between hostile acts directed against the oppressor and indiscriminate acts of violence and brigandage committed against innocent members of the population.

Individual readers will no doubt have their own views as to whether our society is one in which good order and moral conduct remain generally desirable, or whether it is so irremediably evil that a collapse into chaos and strife could only lead to an improvement.

Though armies and police forces may make a considerable contribution to the maintenance of good order in the state, it is doubtful whether a peaceful and stable society would be achieved by their means alone. As an alternative and supplement to overt coercion, therefore, it obviously makes sense to bring up the young so that their actions do not bring them into conflict with other members of society; so that they conform to accepted customs and practices, respect established authorities, the rights of others and so on. This is clearly an attractive proposition as it leads to less open conflict, is less dangerous and probably less costly and more efficient than attempting to maintain constant surveillance (Bourdieu and Passeron, 1970).

The task of bringing the young to conform to the ways of society may be approached in a variety of different manners. One possibility might be to employ a fairly rigorous regime of socialization in which those who deviated from the required norms were simply brought back sharply into line, without a great deal of explanation. In that way children might quite quickly learn that certain things were just not acceptable, and were not worth attempting. Alternatively we might indoctrinate a whole system of

74

beliefs, values and ideals to justify the way our society was run. In that way we might even engage the idealism and highest aspirations of young people in support of our aims.

There are, however, both moral and practical objections to either of these procedures which have little regard to the autonomy of the pupil or his evaluation of his own conduct. They involve the older generation, or certain educationally influential members of the older generation, in choosing how others shall live and eventually controlling the future development of society from beyond the grave. The least evil likely to follow from this is moral stagnation, with today's conventions continuing to bind the conduct of future generations, in situations to which they are no longer appropriate. More serious, perhaps, is the fact that values thus heteronomously acquired are notoriously unreliable in situations of novelty and change. The conduct of Spartans abroad, public schoolboys on rugger tours and convent pupils during their first university term are frequently quoted in this connection, as is the violence and confusion which often follows the collapse of authoritarian regimes.

Apart from coercion, mere socialization and indoctrination there remains a fourth possible approach, namely a programme of genuinely moral education. The possible riposte that one man's moral education is simply another's indoctrination should not be taken too seriously. The term indoctrination has been variously interpreted (see Snook, 1972). It may simply be seen as the putting out of a set of spurious beliefs supportive of a particular set of political interests. Or it may be more closely defined (as by White, 1970 and Degenhardt, 1976) as the inculcation of certain belief systems in such a way that they cannot easily be questioned or criticized. Often, no doubt, the two processes go hand in hand. For our purposes, the distinguishing feature of moral education, as opposed to other approaches to the guidance and control of conduct we have considered, is its essentially conscious and non-exploitative character.

It is assumed that a morally educated person is one who understands that others have interests which are as real and important as his own, and is prepared to act on this view. If we are genuinely concerned with moral education, rather than yet another brand of indoctrination, this reference to understanding is crucial. It is not sufficient to say, with Peters (1974, p. 253), that a moral person is 'someone committed to the impartial treatment of the interests of others'. For such a commitment could be engendered by indoctrinatory means. To insist on the element of understanding implies that the pupil will have come to this conviction through a process of experience and interaction with others, as well as by such means as discussion, reflection and so on. Of course, the task of the moral educator, unlike that of the indoctrinator, is an essentially hazardous one. If we are concerned with genuinely open discussion and critical reflection, rather than with some stage-managed form of substitute for it, we must entertain the possibility that our pupil will come to radically different conclusions from our own. In principle, he may perfectly well conclude that the wishes of some revered authority figure or the prescriptions of a certain religion are of overriding importance, or that the only thing that matters is to look after number one.

To place any confidence in the process of moral education, therefore, one has to think it actually is the case that everyone has interests that are of comparable importance, and also that a process of open-minded reflection will lead people to this conclusion. If one turns out to be wrong, then society will have to fall back – as it is bound to do – upon more coercive measures to protect its citizens.

Thoroughgoing relativists will, no doubt, continue to see the notion of everyone's interests being equally important as ideological, on a par with 'The King's authority comes from God' or 'A woman's place is in the home'. Extreme rightists will also see it as an attempt to 'shackle the strong' and prevent the *Übermensch* from taking 'that which is his due' from the lesser mortals around him. The notion that everyone's interest is of equal importance has the advantage, however, that it is readily understood and rationally defensible. It is incapable of providing moral justification for the exploitation of one individual or group of individuals by another – though it must be admitted that in practice the procedure of majority voting, which derives support from it, may be used to suppress the interests of minorities.

A morally educated person, as opposed to one who has been brought to conformity by some other process, does not refrain from stealing because, in some transcendental sense, 'theft is wrong' but because he perceives that there is no justification for appropriating something which another has created or obtained for his own use. He does not abuse his position on the local council to favour his own business interests, because he sees that the voters would not have elected him if they had known this to be his intention. If he does not break promises or other commonly accepted rules of conduct it is because he sees that he himself profits from the fact that others keep them, and understands that there is no reason why exceptions should be made in his own case.

This does not mean that he will not act in his own interests. He may compete for a post or a contract with the same vigour as anyone else, but only within the same rules as he regards as binding on others. He will obey the just and reasonable practices of his society, not unthinkingly out of habit or because it is the 'done thing' but because others rely on his obedience, just as he relies on theirs. Though he usually follows existing custom, he does so from choice (though he may not make a conscious choice every time he acts). He is therefore in a position to act in a principled way when established practices conflict, or are inappropriate on a particular occasion.

Such an attitude to the rules and practices of orderly, civilized society implies a knowledge of circumstances and consequences and an understanding of both the point of particular practices and the nature of moral action. This emphasis on knowledge and understanding makes the aim an appropriate one to educators. Like all aims, that of moral education is incapable of exhaustive achievement, but is nonetheless a highly practical undertaking.

We are unlikely to produce a society of saints, and may even not wish to do so. Coercive sanctions may remain constantly necessary for some individuals and even the generally well-intentioned may need to be guided by the knowledge that certain actions will simply not be tolerated. Nevertheless, a society in which the goal of moral education has been pursued with only partial success will be a better place to live in than one in which it is disregarded.

There is supposed to be something of a problem or paradox in the notion of moral education. This lies in the fact that though reasons for acting morally can be rationally argued, the commitment to do so cannot be rationally acquired. It seems to be generally agreed (Peters, 1974, p. 255) that moral education is unlikely to be successful unless this commitment is acquired long before the individual has reached the stage of being able to appreciate the rules he has to obey. Paradoxically, therefore, the moral educator must begin the process destined to culminate in moral autonomy by obliging the child to obey rules he cannot yet understand.

Whether or not young children really understand as little as this argument implies, the paradox does not seem fatal to the idea of moral education. If it is a fact that children must pass through a stage of simple obedience or one in which rules are thought to be absolute, so be it. There seems no great evil in a temporary non-rational commitment to a way of behaving which the individual would most likely see to be rationally desirable if he were in a position to do so. The only important thing is that, having got the individual to conform, we should not then omit the critical stage of reflection on the grounds that, since the young person now conforms to our wishes, there is nothing to be gained from carrying the process of moral education any further.

Ideally, the process would seem to be that the individual first becomes committed to certain ways of behaviour in terms of his own particular level of understanding, but later comes to sort out the various anomalies and contradictions and abandons certain rules that no longer seem justified. Though the initial commitment may not be rational, it is reason that determines which commitments are to survive.

It is difficult to see how moral education as characterized above can be anything but a laudable educational aim. It is beneficial to a reasonably just society that it should have citizens who not only obey most of its rules, but do so intelligently, reflecting upon them, adopting them and refining them in the light of changing circumstances.

The moral educator cannot be accused of inducing a state of conformity for the benefit of society to the detriment of the individual. For the morally educated person is only brought to obey rules which he chooses to obey after rational reflection in a society in which he too benefits from the moral conduct of others.

The question of exactly how a moral person should conduct himself in a grossly unjust and oppressive society is a complex one which cannot be satisfactorily dealt with here. Morality certainly does not require one to allow oneself to be robbed and cheated by conforming to standards of honesty one knows others will break. There is, however, a long tradition of argument to the effect that, far from being a negative constraint, having been brought up to be moral is to be seen as a considerable benefit. This is not simply the naive claim that honesty is in some way the 'best policy', for at a certain level it may well not be. Nor is the point the idealist one that the individual achieves some form of self-realization through devoting himself to the highest good of his community (White,

1978, p. 8). Yet if we are very concerned for someone's well-being – as concerned as we are for our own – in the way that adults are often concerned for that of the younger generation, we should certainly want them to grow up able to take care of themselves and look after their own interests. But we should not wish them to grow up egoistic, mendacious or cruel. We should regret such an outcome, not for our own sake – because we feared being abandoned or knocked on the head in our old age – but for theirs. We should feel that they had somehow lost out. Should we not?

There is a final consideration. Even if being morally educated means that the individual is sometimes worse off as a result of considering the interests of others equally with his own, the educator need feel no qualms of conscience on his behalf. For he will only do this when he ought to do so and, furthermore, when he himself decides that he ought. This would certainly not be so in the case of someone who conformed to the norms and customs of his society as a result of indoctrination, socialization or straight coercion.

It will be recalled that our consideration of moral education arises in the context of our dicussion as to how society might be made more law-abiding and orderly. In this context the public demand is usually for socialization rather than moral education. The requirement is for conformity rather than moral reform or innovation. When parents, industrialists, and politicians 'blame the teachers' or 'hold parents responsible' for the ills of society they most emphatically do *not* want youngsters whose moral education leads them to demand better treatment for homosexuals, become indignant at the slaughter of animals or refuse employment in factories making white bread (White, 1982, p. 105), weapons systems or tobacco products.

In a fairly just society, successful moral education ought to result in a degree of law and order, since a moral person will perceive the rightness of conforming to just laws and possibly even to some unjust ones, rather than commit greater injustice or do greater harm by flouting them. In so far as injustice remained, such a person would be committed to work for change through resistance and protest, including symbolic acts of non-conformity if necessary. There can be no guarantee that such activities will not lead to conflict and even violence, for the defenders of injustice will necessarily wish to suppress them. Certainly, there will be accusations of immorality, subversion, lack of respect for law and order, lack of moral fibre, political indoctrination by teachers and so on. The latter, it may even be said, are paid, not to try to reform society by preaching their own values, but simply to pass on the values we have.

That teachers, or anyone else, should attempt to improve society may seem to have overtones of arrogance and paternalism. Yet it can scarcely be right to refrain from so doing when the opportunity lies readily to hand. Only those who would themselves be prepared to refrain from changing society in directions that seemed desirable to them can demand that we should refrain from attempting to reform society. And this certainly excludes most of those who are inclined to criticize teachers for their reforming zeal.

Actually, however, we are not strictly concerned with social reform being pursued by teachers themselves, but by their morally educated ex-pupils. There is no question of the teachers attempting to achieve their own political aims by using their pupils instrumentally to this end. For to educate morally is not to commit individuals to certain kinds of action, but to place them in a position to choose what seems the morally right course of action for themselves.

Some people may feel that this is rather splitting hairs, and that moral education remains subversive; and so indeed it is. For this reason, conspicuously successful moral educators have sometimes ended up drinking hemlock, or swinging from a cross.

Chapter Eight

Equality

Elsewhere (Wringe, 1984) I have discussed ways in which educators may be expected to contribute to the task of rendering society more democratic and (pp. 43–64) have particularly examined the vexed and complex issue of equality of educational opportunity. In the present chapter I am no longer concerned with equality of opportunity but with equality *tout court*. This is a more important and all-embracing aim, for if a society contained only a few social slots in which it were possible to have a satisfactory life, it would be of little comfort to other members of that society that the opportunities to obtain those positions had, in some sense, been equal. Our concern here is therefore with structural inequalities in society rather than with the identities and biographical details of those who occupy the various positions in the structure.

That it is a legitimate aim of teachers and those who formulate educational policy to attempt to render society more equal is not universally agreed. We must begin by dealing with one not uncommon line of argument (see e.g. Cooper, 1980, pp. 1–29) to the effect that the notion of equality itself is in some way vague, meaningless or incoherent. An equal society is here taken to be quite simply one in which there are not wide disparities in either material wealth or in power and status. In such a society, some are not automatically at the beck and call of others, either in virtue of economic necessity or because deference is thought to be automatically owed by the members of one category of individuals to those of another.

In our introductory chapter we suggested that for something to be a legitimate educational aim it should first be desirable in general terms; that teachers should be in a position to promote such an

81

aim as part of their work as educators, and that it should not conflict too disasterously with other well-established educational aims.

For many, the issue of whether a more equal society is itself desirable has long been settled beyond all further discussion. Such a view may be justified by the observation (cf. Locke, 1689–90, II.2.4, p. 309) that no one has any reason to regard himself as being of less consideration than anyone else, or accept a set of social arrangements that bear this implication. In recent times, however, a number of objections have been raised both to the principle of equality, and to some of the arguments that have been put forward in favour of promoting it.

'The Existence of Poverty is not an Argument against inequality'

It is a time-honoured part of the rhetoric in favour of greater equality to describe vividly the pitiful condition of some individuals – farm labourers, factory workers, or starving African children – and contrast this with the lives of those living in superfluous, often vulgar affluence. Opponents of equality, however, claim that this is not a valid argument in favour of equality at all. The fact that people are starving is certainly a reason for feeding them, but equality has nothing to do with it. That people are starving is supposed to be reason for feeding them, not on grounds of equality, but of pity and common humanity. Since there are already sufficient grounds for feeding people, arguments about equality are redundant and may even appear frivolous (Cooper, 1975, p. 121).

The point of this manoeuvre is that, if we accept that affluence and poverty side by side are relevant to each other, it is difficult to avoid the conclusion that together they represent an injustice in the way resources are distributed. It is equally hard to avoid feeling that such a situation ought to be remedied right away – if necessary by the simplistic and obvious device of forcibly taking resources from where they are superfluous, and transferring them as quickly as possible to where they are desperately needed. If, however, we say that for example starvation is a bad state of affairs which ought to be remedied, without reference to the affluence of others, we turn a matter of justice, which we are under an obligation to deal with straight away, into one of charity. We ought all of us – rich and less rich – to be generally charitable and help those in distress. But we have no obligation to help these particular sufferers on this particular occasion. We should be praised for doing so, but neither we nor anyone else can be blamed if we do not. No one is perfect and provided we sometimes act charitably towards others in distress we may continue to consider ourselves virtuous and humane. In technical terms, a duty of perfect obligation (to right an injustice here and now) is transformed into one of imperfect obligation, to which we should all attend, but at times and on occasions of our own choosing.

The manoeuvre is scarcely convincing, for our response to the distribution of wealth in the world is not merely sorrow that deprivation should exist, but indignation at the social and economic arrangements which enable it to do so when others might prevent it. In so far as such a grossly unequal distribution of the world's resources continues it reflects a system of values according to which the whims, pleasures and ostentation of some are more important than the basic needs, or even the lives, of others. To this extent, the issue is not merely one of poverty, but genuinely one of inequality – not merely inequality of wealth, but inequality of regard, for some individuals are quite literally perceived as being persons of such comparatively little importance that even their extreme needs merit no consideration.

'Inequality is Necessary to Economic Prosperity'

Opponents of equality may argue that without differences in wealth and power economic activity would grind to a halt. Incentives are supposed to be necessary if individuals are to be motivated to devote their energies to the production of goods. If the rich were less rich, so the argument goes, the poor would be a good deal poorer. How can we expect those who 'have the talent' to create wealth if we do not reward them by enabling them to become even more affluent? How can we expect the workers to work with real commitment, if they know that ultimately they are cushioned against the threat of destitution? Supposedly, this is a hard-headed economic argument so that those without expertise in that field may hesitate to challenge it. In fact, however, it is an argument about human motivation and values. Such an argument only gets going in a society that is already unequal and in which those with the power to 'create wealth' are comfortably off. Clearly such people cannot be driven on by the threat of penury, for it is supposed that their security is assured. Equally, the poor are not to be encouraged by the prospect of great affluence, for not only would the benefits of higher production have to be spread too thinly to make any difference, but also the benefits of 'getting on' and acquiring more wealth lose their point if they are too widely spread. The point of being better off is the advantage it gives one in purchasing the services of others, or in competing with them for the purchase of goods.

Even if we accepted the primacy of economic motivation, however, it is far from clear that workers and management need to be motivated in such obviously unequal ways. There is, on the contrary, no reason why the power to make decisions that lead to the production of wealth needs to be in the hands of people who are already more comfortably off than others. Indeed, it might be argued that if poverty continues to be tolerated it is because it only has to be endured by the poor. If on the other hand the management of British industry has recently shown a greater sense of urgency than hithero, it just might be because of the realization that unemployment is capable of affecting executives as well as manual workers. The motivation of fear, if it operates at all, would be effective whether or not managers received substantially greater material rewards than those they managed.

A more profound objection to the argument for economic inequality as an incentive, however, is that it assumes that economic gain is the only effective human motivator. Possibly it is, but this is not something which economists do or can demonstrate. It is an assumption of economics as a discipline that rational individuals will act so as to increase their economic advantage. Unfortunately, this theoretical assumption often comes to be regarded either as a statement of fact, or as a prescription, so that acting for other motives is looked upon as 'irrational' or even irresponsible or 'wet'.

Significantly, even in the management of commercial enterprises themselves there has, for some years now, been a move away from theories of scientific management stressing economic gain as a motivation. Instead, modern management theory may recognize the importance of human relations and group norms in determining how hard people work. Alternatively, a desire for fulfilment and self-motivation may provide an explanation (Handy, 1985, pp. 26–34). If such motivations are at all effective – and go-ahead commercial enterprises would hardly take them seriously if they were not – then the argument that the only possible alternatives to inequality are lethargy and economic decline comes to look less convincing. Even if it were useful to signal recognition of extra commitment or extra talent by means of some extra financial reward, it is far from obvious that the wide inequalities of wealth and poverty that currently exist in the world are necessary.

'Equality is Boring and Coercive'

It is sometimes held that a society which was more equal would be less agreeable to live in. Such a society might perhaps be a prey to drab conformity, oppressive, and destructive of freedom. Athens (based on slavery) and France under the old regime are often cited as inegalitarian societies in which intellect and the arts flourished. But individual examples prove nothing. Sparta also had its slaves and South Africa is not culturally distinguished.

No doubt there are rich people who despise the mediocrity of the common herd and find people poorer than themselves dreary, grey or earnest. No doubt, release from the need to earn a living, plus a spot of extra cash, enables some people to engage in glamorous pursuits, travel, purchase interesting possessions or indulge in engaging eccentricities. It is not, however, clear whether rich people really are more interesting, or are merely so to other rich people with whom they may share common concerns and common experience. If the non-rich really do tend to be boring it is not clear whether this is a necessary effect of having a modest income, or whether it results from the universal striving for greater affluence which is the characteristic of an unequal society, but from which the really wealthy are released. If, in an unequal society, only the rich have access to those things that make for an interesting life, this would seem to constitute one more rather than one less reason for distributing such opportunities more widely.

In any case, it is odd to attach such importance to the need to be interesting compared to the evils of an unequal society. One needs, after all, to be quite well off before boredom becomes a major problem. The notion that a more equal society would have to be totalitarian and oppressive is based on the assumption that people are 'naturally' different in their talents and abilities and that a great deal of coercion would have to be exercised to prevent these differences from manifesting themselves.

In part, this argument rests on the notorious error (or debating trick) of confusing equality with sameness, and accusing egalitarians of wanting the latter. In fact, however, someone committed to a more equal society need not be in the least bit worried about the diversity of human talents, or even about modest differences in reward and recognition that such diversity might bring.

What will be of more concern is the way in which differences in wealth and power, which may indeed have had their origin in special abilities or extra effort, are systematically widened over a whole lifetime, not to say from one generation to another. Someone who is just slightly richer or more powerful will tend to be in an advantageous bargaining position in his dealings with others. He has more pressures to exert and more favours to trade. What is centrally of concern to the person committed to social equality is the fact that where differences of wealth and power are wide, individuals will enjoy (or suffer) different qualities of life, life choices and even life expectations (Honderich, 1976, pp. 1–44) to a degree not justified by any differences in desert.

To speak of such differences as a gain in 'freedom' is ludicrous. In widely unequal society the poor are constantly obliged to serve the whims and projects of the rich and must constantly submit to constraint, not to mention indignity and humiliation, to obtain what they need, or even to survive. Of course *some* have more freedom than they would in an egalitarian society. But to adapt an important distinction made by Cooper (1980, p. 53), someone committed to 'more freedom' as a political ideal usually wants to see a distributional increase in freedom – that is, more people being free in the way that the most free were before – rather than an ontological increase in which *some* people are freer than *anyone* was before. This latter ideal might have sinister overtones indeed.

There are further ways in which inequality is likely to lead to more coercion rather than greater freedom, as well as to other undesirable social consequences including violence and social unrest. Defenders of inequality often claim that egalitarian demands are motivated by envy. Let us suppose that this is true, and concede that the emotion of envy is not an edifying one. This, however, would seem to provide little support for inequality, for envy is perfectly natural, if not actually justified, in an unequal society in which advantages of wealth and power are clearly valued, if not actually flaunted. There is little cause for envy among equals.

The underprivileged may not only envy the better-off but also seek to get their hands on their possessions, either by individual criminality or by revolution. Inequality, especially in the modern world in which the have-nots have the means of knowing what the haves have, is a constant stimulus to and, in many cases, a perfectly good justification for social unrest. In consequence, inequality is necessarily accompanied by a whole panoply of forces to protect the advantages and possessions of the privileged, and this rapidly becomes an apparatus of oppression. It is a small step from a police force or private security organization employed to protect the property of richer citizens from robbery and vandalism, to armed para-military riot police employed to contain the population of troublesome areas with tear gas, baton-charges and ultimately firearms. That inequality leads to more oppression rather than to greater freedom is all too apparent in the inegalitarian regimes of both East and West.

If this all seems somewhat distant from the classroom, it must be borne in mind that schooling is an important part of the process by which the differentiation between those who are destined to be affluent and influential and those who are not takes place. Schools are not the only agencies operating in this way. Families and neighbourhood communities may be even more influential and, dare one say it, there may also be inherent differences of ability and temperament. Nevertheless, schools, by virtue of their organizational, curricular and other policies may compound and amplify these differences or – if such is their aim – take deliberate steps to avoid doing so.

Various recent changes in the organization of schooling have been made with precisely this latter intention. The move to comprehensive education, efforts to develop successful modes of mixed ability teaching, and the establishment of a substantial common core curriculum are cases in point. So are efforts to abolish an exclusive private sector in education.

It should be stressed that such policies are not undertaken to 'impose equality' as their detractors often claim but to avoid processes which amplify existing inequalities. In this respect the move to comprehensive education was not so much itself a piece of 'social engineering' as the dismantling of a previous piece of social engineering, the tripartite system, whose prime function was to differentiate between individuals in terms of their future social destinies.

Grammar schools – and this is even truer of schools in the private sector – frequently went to some pains to ensure that their pupils not only advanced further in their studies, but also studied (or avoided studying) a particular range of subjects as well as learning to behave, dress and speak in ways that sharply distinguished them from others. Even much later in life those who have had a grammar or public school education are fairly easily identifiable, not simply in virtue of their competences but because of their speech and bearing. It is not too much of an exaggeration to say that they are frequently seen (even if they do not see themselves) as belonging to a category of individuals entitled to special consideration.

Not having studied certain subjects such as a modern language or Latin often served as an occupational or educational filter, even though candidates were unlikely to use a foreign language in their later work or courses of study. The point was that having studied or not studied these particular subjects served as a convenient shibboleth, enabling social distinctions to be disguised as differences in ability and attainment. In like manner, having studied for a different set of examinations (the old O-level as opposed to CSE, irrespective of the level of pass achieved) served to distinguish between pupils from different bands of the comprehensive school. Significantly, the CSE examination was virtually never taken in public schools, even by pupils for whom the O-level course was clearly unsuitable and who stood little hope of achieving a pass in it.

To be a teacher committed to equality as an aim is to be aware of such policies and practices in schools, and to be committed to reducing their divisive effects. It is, however, not merely these major organizational arrangements that emphasize and progressively amplify differences between pupils. There are many ways of conveying the message that some pupils are more valued than others, may naturally expect more consideration, and have interests which must be protected when there is competition for attention or resources. These ways include the allocation of rooms and staff, expenditure on books and equipment and, of course, the quality of teacher response and interaction in the classroom. They also include the everyday teacher language of top, middle and bottom sets, A, B and C bands, reference to moving pupils 'up' and 'down' and so on. The message is also conveyed by which achievements, and more especially whose achievements, are recognized and celebrated and whose are ignored.

The problem that anyone concerned with equality faces in dealing with these matters is that they are easily represented as trivial or petty. The changes of class names to, for example, 1J and 1S (Miss Jones's first-year class, Mr Smith's first-year class) instead of 1A and 1D is often regarded with irony or even criticized as hypocrisy. The school may be accused of attempting to deny 'reality' as if the reality of A, B and C streams were more than a social construct. Yet it is these small indications of attitude which create the school ethos and may more effectively mediate our value assumptions than more explicit attempts at value education. In the matter of equality, attitudes are supremely important, for it is these that determine the extent to which advantage and deference is expected and demanded as a right by the privileged and conceded as reasonable and proper by the remainder of the population.

Though values may be more effectively caught through the general school ethos than imparted through explicit teaching, there may nevertheless seem to be a case for the deliberate presentation of equality as a value through whatever modes of moral education the school employs.

Direct exhortation may be crude and ineffectual, but schools have not hesitated to commend models of courage, inventiveness, piety, industry or patriotism, to name but a few of the qualities different societies have valued and sought to encourage in the young. Those who have fought, often died, and in many places continue to do so, for the sake of equality may also seem worthy of presentation to the young for their approval and emulation.

No indoctrination of controversial political values is here being proposed. In so far as equality is one of the most fundamental and – outside the academic world – widely acknowledged values of our society, those who oppose its teaching are way out of line. No politician, even of the extreme right (except in South Africa), stands up and openly speaks against equality. Those who have inegalitarian policies to propose will normally do so in terms of some other value such as securing the economic base, or attempt to show that in some round-about way such policies will ultimately benefit all.

Nor is it proposed that the value of equality should be taught in such a way that it will not be challenged or criticized, for the more passionately and critically the values of equality and its alternatives are discussed, the better.

If the drive for more social equality is both morally desirable in itself and something which both practically can and legitimately may be promoted within the educational process, it remains to consider how far it conflicts with other acknowledged educational aims.

Provided equality is not interpreted as sameness, there is no reason why the aim of producing a society in which all are valued equally should be inimical to those aims considered earlier, which directly benefit the individual and favour his personal development. On the contrary, such aims are more compatible with an education suitable to a society of equals than that necessary in unequal societies of the past when both rich and poor alike had to be schooled in ways thought appropriate to their station. Only those whose happiness and fulfilment is to be found in flaunting their superiority or exercising their power over others are likely to feel that their personal development is inhibited by an education aimed at promoting a sense of equality and mutual respect.

It is difficult to see how such an education can be in conflict with the aim of developing each individual's personal autonomy. The contrary, indeed, would seem to be the case in so far as respect for one's own equal value and that of others is rationally justifiable. Traditional deference to the authority of others, subordination to their superior power or simply a sycophantic desire to please one's betters are obvious enemies of autonomy. Rejection of any such inclinations may be seen as a necessary part of the character of an autonomous individual.

Possibly those who have been taught to see themselves as the equals of others may be less good workers than those who have not – at least from the point of view of those who employ them. This, however, is not entirely obvious. In a relatively complex post-industrial world employers may regard docility and dependence as less valuable than initiative and self-confidence. Staff training and development procedures may be designed to produce these latter qualities in many go-ahead organizations.

As we saw earlier in this chapter, there are reasons for thinking that an equal society is at least as likely to be governed by law and order as one that is unequal. It will also become clear that equality is far from incompatible with the values of justice discussed in the following two chapters.

Possibly more serious attention should be given to the conflict which some writers claim to have seen between the aim of promoting social equality and that of encouraging educational excellence. Such writers lay particular stress on the special place in education of subjects (both artistic and intellectual) in which great care and effort by teachers and pupils may lead to a high level of performance. Such subjects are often those used to identify those pupils who are destined for the most valued social positions.

As we saw, however, for someone committed to equality it is not differences in intellectual achievement which are undesirable but the different rewards and levels of social status we choose to link to them. That we should do this is a matter of decision, not of logic or necessity. Talented artists and scholars themselves may be extremely modest individuals who do not always see their abilities as entitling them to material benefits or special privileges. They may, indeed, often be scornful of fellow artists or scholars who are more interested in outward rewards than the internal standards of their art or discipline. Anyone sincerely committed to excellence for its own sake, rather than for the sake of the honours and extrinsic rewards it brings, must necessarily take the same view.

To value certain kinds of achievement is not simply to value their highest expression in unique individuals, but to value their beginnings and the process of their development as well as encouraging their greatest possible improvement whenever they are found. There is no contradiction in logic between valuing the achievements of all pupils and valuing excellence. Indeed, it is difficult to see how one could value any form of excellence without also valuing the elementary stages on the road towards its accomplishment.

Only at the contingent level of resourcing may there seem to be some conflict. One might, perhaps, have to choose between providing science teaching for all pupils, or providing superb laboratories and the most excellent teachers for a small number of gifted pupils. Unless it is certain that the latter policy would ultimately prove self-defeating it must be admitted that some conflict may be unavoidable, as it would in the case of any two aims whose implementation made calls on limited resources.

This is not to say that the pursuit of either equality or of excellence is an invalid aim, but simply that neither should be pursued exclusively of the other. No doubt a society committed to both would insist that its educational resources should be dis-

tributed fairly evenly, otherwise its commitment to equality would be meaningless. But it might still set aside some resources to foster exceptional talent or enthusiasm, especially where the individual himself was prepared to make exceptional sacrifices of time and effort. This would seem particularly acceptable if the talent in question were widely beneficial to the community at large and not linked to obvious material advantage for its possessor.

Though there must clearly exist a certain vitalizing tension with such a policy, it is difficult to see it as entirely destructive of either aim. Such a line of thinking might enable the government of the Soviet Union not only to countenance but to give its positive support to the most distinguished of all ballet companies.

92

Chapter Nine

Justice

Equality and justice are not synonymous but there are important connections between the two and it will be argued that justice comes down to a kind of equality in the end. At a superficial level, however, there are a number of distinctions to be made. Among these is that saying that two people are being treated equally is a statement of fact (if it is true) and it is a further question as to whether this state of affairs is desirable. But if we agree that a certain way of treating them is just, no further justification is required, though we may always argue as to whether it is just or not.

In recent years two influential accounts of the concept of justice have appeared. Neither of these seems ultimately tenable and neither is centrally concerned with education. It is necessary, however, to give some attention to the accounts of both Nozick (1974, pp. 149–231) and Rawls (1973), since both accounts have enthusiastic adherents and may play an important part in discussions about the distribution of social and educational goods.

A feature of Nozick's conception of justice is that it is perfectly consistent with the widest possible inequalities in the distribution of material goods, and is therefore often invoked by those opposed to the promotion of equality as an educational or social aim. According to Nozick, goods may be justly come by in three ways:

(1) When someone takes some previously unowned object or material from 'the state of nature' and transforms it into a usable or valuable object by his own efforts (justice in acquisition).
(2) When some justly owned good is voluntarily transferred (given, sold, bequeathed) to someone else (justice in transfer).

(3)   As compensation for some earlier act of injustice.

Such a conception of justice is easily reconcilable with extreme inequalities of wealth and power. Some people may be in no position to take what they need from the state of nature while others, by a series of 'just transfers', may accumulate wealth in superfluity. If some starve to death while others live in plenty that is unfortunate but, according to Nozick, no injustice.

There is nothing to prevent those in possession of goods from increasing the differential in wealth by employing the efforts of others who 'voluntarily' give their labour, however disadvantageous the terms, rather than starve. The state may legitimately levy taxes for the purpose of defence and policing to protect the property of those who 'justly' own it from the depradations of those who do not, for this is something to which the possessors of property must rationally agree to as being in their interests. It is, however, an important part of Nozick's argument that injustice is involved in any attempt to impose taxes for the purposes of providing for the welfare of the needy. This would be to deprive someone against his will of goods which he had justly obtained.

This account is an attempt to recycle some of the liberal natural rights theories of the seventeenth and eighteenth centuries, which attempt to define a just society as that which would arise naturally among reasonable beings living freely and independently in a state of nature. It is an assumption of such theories that injustice can only come about as a result of individual unjust acts – that is, acts resulting in people being obliged to do something, or being deprived of something, without their consent. Yet clearly this is not the only way in which injustice can arise. If I do not choose to speak to a colleague, that is no injustice. I am not obliged to speak to anyone if I do not wish to. Others may make the same claim. But if everyone refuses to speak to an individual (as each would individually appear to be entitled to do) he may rightly claim that he is a victim of collective persecution.

Secondly, according to the natural rights tradition, property is indeed acquired in the first place by taking something from the 'state of nature' and 'mixing it with one's labour'. The property then rightfully belongs to the agent because it is only his labour that transforms it into something of value. But it was an important proviso of this theory that one may only take from the state of nature so long as there is 'enough and as good left in common for others' (Locke, 1689–90, II.5.27, p. 239). Locke and others writing in that tradition had little regard for the finite nature of the world's resources. Yet if the destitute in the twentieth century cannot 'take from the state of nature' to nourish themselves by their efforts, it is because most of what was worth taking has already been taken by others, and precious little is left. The position of the destitute is therefore the result of at least some acts of injustice by those who have taken from the state of nature without leaving either enough or as good behind. Since it is, however, difficult to identify which particular acts these were and most present owners seem to have come by their goods by legitimate acts of transfer, the destitute have no one against whom they can claim just restitution. It must be said that Nozick recognizes and discusses this problem, but concedes that he does not succeed in resolving it (pp. 178–82).

Thirdly, Nozick also readily concedes that the just processes he describes would hardly account for the present distribution of goods in the real world (p. 152). His central concern is simply to show that any egalitarian or other 'patterned' redistribution would be bound to be unjust, as he has explained the term. What he does not show, however, is that any such redistribution would, even in his own terms, be more unjust than the present distribution, resulting from many past acts of injustice of one kind or another and compounded by a systematic exploitation of an advantageous bargaining position (see Wringe, 1981b, pp. 72–3 for 'unequal contracts'). Needless to say, Nozick's acknowledgement that his account of justice does not necessarily relate to the present distribution of goods does not prevent his name from being invoked by those who wish to defend that distribution against those who might wish to change it.

In a second account of the concept of justice, Rawls (1973) argues that a just society is one which a rational person would choose if he did not know what his own position in that society was to be. It is assumed that the rational person will choose a society in which he would not be too badly placed if the person who occupied the least favoured role in that society were himself. Indeed, so Rawls argues, he would choose the arrangement in which the least favoured person were as well off as possible. The insistence that the rational person is not to know what his own position (this includes his own tastes, inclinations and abilities) is to be is Rawls's ways of expressing the principle that a just society is one which would be chosen by an impartial person – that is, one who does not allow his choice to be swayed by considerations of personal advantage. The device of insisting that the person who is to choose the distribution of goods and advantages in society is not to know what his own position is to be, and therefore to fear that his may be the worst, is akin to one often used by parents for teaching the notion of 'fair shares' to their children. The child who cuts the cake or divides the fruit receives his or her portion last, and is therefore motivated to share it as absolutely equally as possible.

Rawls's theory, however, is not an argument for equality but an elaborate and often involved justification of inequality and meritocracy for, Rawls argues, in society at large some inequalities may actually be to the advantage of the least fortunate. The obvious case of this would be the offering of financial incentives in industry. This might improve overall productivity so that it would be possible for the least productive and least rewarded person to receive more than he received under the more egalitarian and less efficient arrangement, even though he now receives less than his fellow workers. For Rawls, therefore, the just society is not necessarily an equal society but one in which inequalities are allowed provided they benefit the worst off (p. 60). A rational person, even if he were the worst off of all members of the society, would, Rawls claims, choose such an arrangement in preference to one in which all were equal but all worse off than the least privileged member of an unequal society. It does, of course, look very plausible to suppose that if you said to the complaining underprivileged member of an unequal arrangement 'Look, if you don't accept your unequal position, you will be even worse off than you are now', he would be bound to acquiesce in the status quo. This, in fact, is what is being said when politicians ask the not very well off to accept a policy of tax cuts for the wealthy, coupled with wage restraint or even a measure of unemployment in order to 'preserve the economic base' or 'create the wealth' which makes possible any wages or social benefits at all. The alternative, it is explained, is national bankruptcy and possibly starvation. Much the same argument may be applied in non-economic spheres when authoritarian governments point out that the alternative of chaos and disorder would benefit no one, even the presently most oppressed. It also underlies Hobbes's view that rational individuals are bound to choose absolute monarchy since anything less is sure to degenerate into the war of all against all which no one could prefer.

A defender of Rawls's theory would rightly insist, however, that it may not be invoked in defence of extreme or unnecessary inequalities. For though, even in a grossly exploitative situation, there might be a dramatic worsening in the conditions of the worst off if the existing social structure were simply withdrawn, this does not mean that any and every form of existing social structure is justified. A Greek slave in a kindly family would probably be better off than if he were abandoned to robbers and wild beasts, but this does not justify slavery, for there are many other possible social arrangements under which the slave might be better off, and live safely.

All the same, it is a major weakness of Rawls's theory that once equality or something like it is abandoned as the standard of justice it becomes very difficult (Richards, 1982, p. 152) to know when the 'just' situation *à la* Rawls has been reached. Certain extremes are no doubt ruled out, as in the case of gross deprivation which allows people to starve or die of preventable disease, for people in this situation could not possibly be worse off. It also rules out superfluous luxury (in the presence of great need) or arbitrary tyranny which contributes nothing to the good of the worst off. But there is no way of telling precisely which inequalities would be justified.

The privileged would always argue – as they do in fact – that their particular privileges are, by one extended process of economic causality or another, essential to the well-being of the least well off, and would therefore figure in the scheme of things chosen by the rational individual from behind the famous veil of ignorance. There could, even in principle, be no way of deciding whether or not this was true, for whether or not a particular act of equalization benefited or harmed the least well off would depend on what else was changed in that society.

It is no answer for the Rawlsian to point out that only the total package which was of most advantage to whoever happened to be the worst off would be acceptable, for there is no possibility of determining which this would be. In the meantime the theory serves to defend particular inequalities depending on what assumptions one makes about what other parts of society it is desirable to change, or not change, to meet the demands of the theory.

Rawls, like many other social philosophers, must make certain assumptions about human nature and human life in order to render his theory plausible. One of these is that there are fairly permanent and irreducible differences in human capacity, and that for these to be deployed efficiently a differential system of rewards is necessary. Rawls, however, does not show (and does not attempt to show) that such a system has an overall beneficial effect on the production of goods in a particular society. One might well imagine that the less well rewarded would be significantly demotivated, while those holding more privileged positions would spend much of their time defending those positions at the expense of their actual effectiveness. There is a plausible radical interpretation of Rawls's so-called difference principle, which, as is clear from the general tenor of his argument, Rawls himself does not take very seriously. This is that the only arrangement according to which the least well off stands the remotest chance of reasonable treatment is one of complete equality, or something close to it. On this interpretation, no inequalities, or only very insignificant ones, are justified by the principle. Possibly, individuals might earn small extra sums for moonlighting or overtime and there might even be small premiums to encourage the development of skills which were in particular demand. In an open and fairly egalitarian society there is no reason to suppose that great differentials would be necessary for this purpose.

The reason that only a regime of approximate equality would allow the Rawlsian principle to be met is as follows. If human nature is such that maximum productivity of social goods can only be ensured by fairly significant differentials in reward, it is not plausible to suppose that those who acquire the most influential positions (by virtue of their special abilities) will consent to benefit only by such inequalities as favour the least fortunate. For if the least fortunate are also the least competent it is certain that they will also be the least politically powerful, as is the case in any real state in the real world. Add to this the difficulties mentioned above, of determining precisely which situation best fulfils the Rawlsian requirement, and the observed tendency of all but the perfectly selfless to interpret doubtful cases to their own advantage, and it is difficult to see how an unequal society can in practice be to the overall advantage of the least fortunate. Only by insisting that society's goods are shared more or less equally is it possible both to increase the total amount of goods at society's disposal, and to ensure that the able, and especially those who have practical and political gifts, do not increase their share to the detriment of the less fortunate and less astute.

Of course, in supposing that the able and well-rewarded will act egoistically I too am making unflattering assumptions about human nature. But I am not obliged to do so. I may concede that the most productive may not be motivated by egoism. But if this is the case, the need for differentials to motivate the most productive disappears. Unlike Rawls, I do not require individuals to be egoistic for one part of my argument and selflessly scrupulous beyond all plausibility for the other.

Rawls's theory is open to attack from both left and right. An egalitarian may object to a system which encourages the most productive to expect differential rewards in return for the greater contribution he is only able to make through the good fortune of being born with greater abilities. Once basic needs are met, being well off in terms of the goods of status and display is comparative rather than absolute. To many, being 'less than equal' might be the worst of all evils (apart from death), especially if this less than equality were supposed to represent the lesser value of one's contribution to society. Opening the weekly wage packet would then be not just a cause of disgruntlement, but deep humiliation.

Objection may also be made from the right. In Rawls's world merit and achievement would only receive reward when this was of instrumental value to the masses. But this, it might be argued, is not justice but base expediency. Those who achieve and contribute more should surely receive more, irrespective of whether it is the least able who benefit from it.

These objections from both left and right spring from an understanding of the concept of justice which is both older and less sophisticated than those of either Nozick or Rawls. According to this concept, to act justly is to treat equals equally and only unequals unequally. As expressed by Carritt (1947, p. 156), the principle requires that we discriminate between individuals on relevant grounds, but on relevant grounds only.

The question of what grounds are relevant must naturally be broached. Birth, race, gender and religion have all been considered grounds for depriving individuals of equal treatment in the past, and progress towards social justice has involved the gradual recognition that these are not acceptable grounds for negating the presumption in favour of equal treatment at all. Need and desert (meriting either punishment or reward), on the other hand, are generally seen as grounds for treating people differently without infringing the principle of justice.

It might be thought that the aim of increasing society's stock of goods and thereby increasing the lot of all (including the least fortunate) justified discriminating in favour of some people to encourage more efficient production. This, however, must be correctly understood. If the extra productiveness is reckoned to be the result of some extra effort or other meritorious act of will on the agent's part, then, provided there are no other ill effects, it is right that he should be rewarded – desert being a morally relevant ground of discrimination. But if the extra productiveness arises from natural ability or good fortune, clearly desert is not involved. We might, nevertheless, wish to show some recognition of exceptional ability – in the way that we award medals and certificates of merit for exceptional specimens at the annual flower show. But this is not justice, but an act of supererogatory celebration. When we reward an exceptional performer in order to ensure that he continues to perform exceptionally, this is not an act of justice, but of policy. The policy may be abandoned or changed in favour of other values and priorities as they become apparent.

The three interpretations of justice we have touched upon each start from a presumption of equality between individuals with none, initially, having special prerogatives or claims. Nozick and Rawls seek to provide justification for possible inequalities, Nozick on grounds of particular acts or transactions, Rawls on grounds of particular talents. The third conception of justice mentioned retains the notion of equality more obviously in evidence and the permitted departures from it may seem more apparent than real. That more should be given to the needy is not inequality but the reduction of an inequality. It may be thought that some ingenuity is required in order to provide a similar justification for the reward of merit. But if merit entails some extra 'giving out' of effort, or something similar, then the reward may perhaps be seen as some form of compensation. Beyond this, reward may be justified as token recognition of actions, virtues and talents we profess to admire and seek to encourage in others.

Where the education service is an organ of public provision it is obviously essential that the good it provides should be distributed justly. In the light of our third account of justice, this does not necessarily mean that it will be distributed entirely equally. There is nothing in such a concept of justice to rule out the possibility of making special provision for those with special needs. It is less clear to what extent extra ability should be met with extra provision. It is difficult to see that such extra provision would be a right demanded by justice and, if made, it would have to be in pursuit of other goals, such as promoting excellence, as suggested in the previous chapter. Unless, of course, certain very able children were unable to learn in ordinary classrooms because they became bored and delinquent. In that case they might be entitled to benefit from the extra provision due to other maladjusted children on grounds of special need.

There ought not only to be justice in the provision of education, but the promotion of a just society is a legitimate and necessary educational aim. There is no truth in the gibe that schools should leave justice to the courts and attend to their own business, which is teaching. If schools are organs of public provision they are no more entitled to pursue policies which lead to injustice than the police, the rates office or the National Health Service. They are under an obligation to review their policies and practices, including curricular policies and classroom practices, to ensure that they are neither unjust in the present, nor likely to give rise to injustice in the future. Content, teaching styles or the communication of attitudes which make it more likely that some or all of a school's pupils will suffer (or inflict) injustice need to be identified and avoided. Needless to say, this includes all educational processes which predispose some sections of the school population to accept unduly low expectations of themselves or needlessly acquiesce in subordinate roles. It also includes the communication of attitudes of superiority and the expectation of privilege in other pupils.

If all this sounds somewhat negative it should be pointed out that much of the work of establishing a just society consists precisely in the removal of causes of injustice. The notion of justice is also an essential part of the value education of pupils, both directly and indirectly as part of the curricular content of schools. It is important that pupils should experience the school as an institution in which they and others are treated justly. The school is the first institution of the state with which future citizens consciously come into contact, and this experience will necessarily determine the expectations they will have and the standards they will demand of other institutions later in life.

Chapter Ten

Justice, Race and Gender

It is widely recognized that our society is unjust in its treatment of women and also of people who are black or brown. It is sometimes held to be naive to conflate discussion of these two forms of injustice, and no doubt this would be true if we were concerned with the psychological causes of prejudice. In terms of their effects and possible remedies, however, there do seem to be sufficient parallels to justify this procedure, which may in itself prove illuminating.

The process of schooling is thought to contribute to both forms of injustice and the possibility also exists that, with suitable reforms, schooling may help to put matters right.

The issues of racism and sexism have produced a plethora of both empirical research and highly polemical writing, and readers who have strong views on these subjects may feel that what follows is cool and passionless. It is hoped, however, that it will be of some small contribution to the causes of social and sexual justice to set out clearly what seem to be the main issues; for confusion and overstatement play too easily into the hands of those, often skilled in the art of advocation, in whose interest it is to deride and oppose these concerns.

The injustice complained of is of two kinds. First, members of the categories in question often do not enjoy the same economic and social advantages that they would enjoy if they were male or white. This claim assumes that a society in which there were significant inequalities would be more just if positions in that society were at least consistently allocated on some such grounds as merit. In earlier chapters we advanced grounds for doubting this, and suggested that a society would only be just if benefits were distributed fairly equally, irrespective of differences between individuals. Clearly, the existence of an equal society would pre-empt questions of both racial and sexual injustice, and no doubt this is what we should be aiming for in the long run. For the purposes of this chapter, however, it is proposed to ignore this wider possibility and concentrate on the complaint that some individuals suffer the double injustice, that they do not receive their due even according to the rules that are supposed to apply in a consistently operating meritocracy.

It will also be noted that neither Nozick's nor Rawls's concepts of justice are helpful here. On Nozick's view it would be perfectly possible to suppose that only white males had had the idea of taking things from the state of nature and mixing them with their labour, or had benefited from just acts of transfer on advantageous terms. If such individuals elected to transfer resources to other categories of persons on less favourable terms – for example, in return for less remunerative forms of work, or positions of social inferiority – that would be their right. It is true that Rawls assumes that the rational individual behind the veil of ignorance would wish occupational rules to be allocated on grounds of merit, but it is not clear that this would be so if it were the case, for example, that the concentration of women in 'caring' but relatively unrewarded roles was most beneficial to the least well off. Only the third conception of justice we considered seems directly and straightforwardly apposite here, for the complaint is that women and coloured people suffer disadvantage on the morally irrelevant grounds of race and sex. Whatever the benefits (to the least favoured or anybody else) of having women or black people in systematically inferior positions, they themselves have done nothing to merit it and are under no moral obligation to accept such a situation.

A second form of racial and sexual injustice often complained of is that the members of the categories in question often suffer insult, humiliation, abuse and even harrassment on account of their sex and race, and that this is often disregarded if not actually compounded by those from whom they might reasonably expect redress. Polemical writers and speakers are able to produce lengthy catalogues of anecdotes, public remarks and incidents showing that women or coloured people are the subject of unfavourable tacit assumptions, their contribution is under-valued and their wrongs and misfortunes treated as if they were of less account than those of other members of society. Often these are so outrageous that they might have been regarded as amusing in less sensitive times. Advertisements for flats without baths, supposedly suitable for coloured families, and husbands' remarks that their wives 'do not work' because there are four children and two large dogs to look after at home are trivial but telling examples. School lessons in history which speak of the 'savages' of Africa or the bringing of 'civilization' to India are others. The fact that the police often seem in no hurry to investigate crimes committed against coloured people, or that judges may see fit to make facetious public remarks about crimes of violence against women are perhaps matters of greater moment.

Institutional Bias in Education

Sexual or racial injustice may result from individual acts of prejudice, but also from what may be termed systematic or institutional bias. This latter phenomenon may take a number of forms but for our purposes it is useful to distinguish between unintentional administrative bias and bias which results specifically from the processes of socialization and education. Conditions of promotion that insisted upon an unbroken record of employment would introduce such a bias against able, experienced and well-qualified women who had taken a short period out of work for family reasons, whether or not the rules were introduced for this purpose.

Institutional bias may occur in the educational system in a number of ways. It is proposed to consider:

(1) the creation of stereotypes and self-images;
(2) invisibility and cultural imperialism;
(3) the placing of unequal barriers in the way of different children's learning.

THE CREATION OF STEREOTYPES AND SELF-IMAGES

This is the process by which different expectations and different norms of behaviour are created in different categories of pupils. Its existence forms part of the argument against all kinds of educational segregation, whether by class, sex, race or whatever, which may

104

lead to the learning of leadership and initiative in one place and conscientious conformity in another. But it is also possible to socialize children differentially without separating them physically. Numerous studies show in detail how the differential socialization of boys and girls takes place. Girls are given dolls and brush-and-dustpan sets to play with, while boys receive tool sets and Lego. At school, in the past at least, boys and girls have been encouraged or even obliged to study different subjects. Subjects leading to practical careers (like physics) may not be taught in a 'girl-friendly' manner or atmosphere. Teachers may show they expect different standards from boys and girls. Boys may be pushed to get their sums right and, with misguided chivalry, girls let more easily off the hook. Boys may be encouraged to compete for teachers' attention while girls quickly learn that it is considered more ladylike to put up one's hand and wait patiently. Above all it appears that girls soon learn that they are not expected to shine too obviously in the presence of their male classmates. Different racial groups may also be socialized according to disadvantageous stereotypes. West Indian children may find that not a great deal is demanded or expected of them academically while their performance on the sports field produces more excitement (Gallop and Dolan, 1981). The precise way in which these expectations are communicated are yet to be identified. The actions, words and responses of teachers obviously play a significant part, but those of other pupils both within and outside the disadvantaged group will no doubt also contribute.

Whatever the processes involved, however, the net result is that some categories of children will tend to achieve less well than others, or achieve in different areas. In consequence, they will be less well placed to compete for advantageous employment. This disadvantage is, of course, added to any actual prejudice that employers and others may be guilty of, and may often serve to justify it.

INVISIBILITY AND CULTURAL IMPERIALISM

Much of what girls learned in traditional history lessons related to the achievement of famous men, whether in winning battles, exploring distant continents or inventing useful pieces of industrial machinery. If women had any part to play it was in supportive and caring roles, like Florence Nightingale, or it was played by women (like Boadicea or Joan of Arc) whose actions were more like those of men anyway. They will have learned that 'Man' is descended from the apes, and that 'Mankind' constantly strives for perfection. Much of what was learned in the sciences and even mathematics seems to relate more or less exclusively to the concerns of men, rather than to their own. Over large areas of the school curriculum the existence of women was scarcely acknowledged.

Children belonging to ethnic minorities may equally have some difficulty in relating to the heroes of history, the families in their reading books, or the characters and issues studied in literature lessons. When human achievements and aspirations are spoken of, people like themselves may be conspicuous by their absence and it would not be surprising if the more perceptive and critical among them were to say 'But what has all this to do with me?'

Quite apart from any disaffection and lesser achievement that may result, this situation already constitutes an injustice in that it disvalues certain groups of people, and subjects them to an education which is not centrally relevant to them. It is, indeed, often suggested that the whole of the school curriculum, being a product of Western culture, is necessarily alien to those from other parts of the world who not only have their own cultural traditions, but also their own standards of logic and rationality. On this view the imposition of a 'Western' curriculum with Western standards and criteria of achievement represents an act of oppression, or even cultural genocide.

In dealing with this issue there are a number of traps to be avoided. An obvious response to the accusation of imposing a 'male' or 'Western' curriculum on those to whom it was not appropriate would be separate educational provision in different institutions. To accede to the demand for separate Islamic schools would be a move in this direction. In general, however, such a retreat towards cultural fragmentation would be disastrous. In the field of race relations the slogan 'separate but equal' has not a happy history and experience has also shown that 'parity of esteem' between different kinds of institution cannot be imposed by fiat. It is also well established (Richards, 1982, pp. 195–8) that where separate activities and separate learnings are undertaken by men and women, those undertaken by women are always disvalued, by women as well as by men.

UNEQUAL EDUCATIONAL BARRIERS

Seen from a certain point of view, the educational system constitutes a kind of hurdles race from which pupils emerge with various qualifications which may lead on to higher education or various levels of employment. To children from non-indigenous families, the hurdles may be more difficult than for others. This is an extension of the well-known argument that working-class children are at a disadvantage at school because they have to learn a whole range of things – facts, idioms and attitudes – which middle-class children and their middle-class teacher take for granted. Many of the things they have already learnt at home simply do not count as educational achievements, and may even have to be painfully unlearnt if they are not to be noted to the child's disadvantage. Children of families from outside the British Isles may suffer the same disadvantage in a more acute form. Language may be an obvious additional barrier, and even where the child appears to communicate fluently he or she may fail to understand what they hear correctly. Differences in speech and writing may simply be perceived and assessed as errors by their teacher, or even taken as a sign of limited general intelligence. Lack of fluency and spontaneity in what may be the child's second or third language may also lead to children's being regarded as 'dim' or unco-operative. There are, of course, many other ways in which ethnic minority children may be at a disadvantage and have to learn what every indigenous child knows already. References in reading books and literary texts to the flora and fauna of the English countryside, to English foods, English daily routines and Christian practices may well be meaningless to them. These things not only constitute an extra burden of learning but constitute unequal barriers in two other ways. First, they are harder to learn and understand than other things because the child has no concrete experience of them. Secondly, the English teacher may take such knowledge for granted and failure to explain may render a whole lesson incomprehensible to some members of the class. Of course, the members of non-indigenous racial groups will possess their own stock of taken-for-granted knowledge and understanding not possessed by indigenous children. But unless the teacher is both sensitive and well-informed these pupils will quickly learn that such things are not 'required knowledge'. They had better be kept quiet about, as reference to them tends to produce incomprehension or ridicule.

Policies for Rectifying Racial and Gender Injustice

In so far as the education system or other institutions place some members of the community at a disadvantage in a competitive society there would appear to exist an obligation to attempt to put matters right. Just how this should be done is not obvious, however, and a number of well-meaning proposals raise their own difficulties either because of their apparent inadequacy (provoking the criticism that they are mere palliatives) or because they themselves are supposed to constitute an injustice towards other social groups. Under this head the following proposals merit some discussion:

(1)   reverse discrimination;
(2)   a policy of 'colour blindness' or 'gender blindness' ('treating them all the same');
(3)   valuing minority cultures ('multicultural education');
(4)   a deliberate policy of anti-racist (or anti-sexist) education.

REVERSE DISCRIMINATION

In addition to outlawing unfair appointment and selection practices, policies have been widely advocated, and in many cases instituted, which give an actual advantage to members of previously disadvantaged groups. This may take the form of demanding lower entry qualifications (e.g. for academic courses) or requiring institutions to employ a certain proportion of black people or women, irrespective of whether better qualified whites or men are available. This practice has been held to be unjust towards the better qualified members of previously more favoured groups who are now supposedly subject to 'unfair' competition (see Dworkin, 1977, pp. 223–39), as well as towards the public at large whose interest is supposed to be best served by appointing or selecting the best available candidates, whoever they may be (Goldman, 1979, pp. 22–64). It may also be held (pp. 142–4) that this practice is against the true interest of the disadvantaged groups concerned since their inferior performance in responsible and demanding roles will reflect badly on their groups as a whole, and would not achieve the object of providing desirable role models for other members of the group. There is also held to be a problem about deciding which groups should benefit from reverse discrimination, since human beings can be classified in numerous ways, and there exists the irony that the most privileged members of underprivileged groups may well be better off than the least privileged members of groups which are generally at an advantage. Proponents of this argument are inclined to invoke the possible case of a black student from an affluent professional background in competition with a white student from a poor family in competition for, say, a university place. On the face of it, the latter might seem to have justification for complaint if the former were chosen, despite having inferior qualifications. Justice, it is claimed, operates between individuals rather than between groups and Goldman (1979, pp. 76–94) argues that reverse discrimination is only justifiable when it can be shown that the member of the advantaged group has *personally* profited from favourable discrimination in the past and that the particular member of the disadvantaged group in question has suffered from it as an individual.

None of the above arguments appear to constitute valid objections to the principle of reverse discrimination as a social policy. It is true that each requires to be taken seriously and considered separately on its merits. At the outset, however, it must be said that they point to a relatively small number of possible, in some cases entirely hypothetical, instances of individual injustices or disadvantages as objections to a policy intended to rectify a kind of injustice whose existence is all but universally admitted, and whose effects are pervasive. It is true that in practice any policy of reverse discrimination may result in anomalies – or potential anomalies – which may be seized upon and derided by its opponents. Such is the complexity of human affairs and the need of law and administration to lay down clear and relatively uncomplicated definitions in advance, that almost any social policy whatsoever may run into problems of this kind. This is not an argument for cynically setting aside the rights of individuals in the name of social expediency, but for promptly taking such broadly justifiable steps as are necessary to mitigate widespread and obvious injustice, and then seeking ways of acting flexibly and intelligently as a kind of 'fine tuning' to deal with any anomalies and the individual injustices to which they give rise.

The general issues of inequality and reverse discrimination may take us some way from the practicalities of the classroom, but educational institutions not only pass on knowledge, but also function as agencies of social selection. Often this process is relatively conscious and deliberate, as when we allocate pupils to different groups, guide them in their choices of courses and careers, or recommend them for employment or higher education. Necessarily, the way in which teachers perform these tasks will to some extent affect the kind of society we have. Teachers cannot therefore remain unaware of the various policy options available in this area, or their implications and the justifications which may be given for them.

TREATING THEM ALL THE SAME

Some well-intentioned and liberal minded teachers – no doubt with perfect sincerity – profess to be colour or gender blind. 'I teach maths, physics, history, RE, or whatever. Boys, girls, black, white – they are all the same to me. I also avoid offensive expressions referring to coloured people and excessive use of the masculine pronoun, provided this can be done without awkwardness or pedantry.'

This is a desirable advance on overtly racist or sexist attitudes but is nevertheless open to a number of criticisms. First, it is these days somewhat implausible for teachers to claim to take no account of important facts about the background, personality and interests of those they are teaching. It can scarcely be irrelevant to the way a teacher goes about the task of engaging interest or otherwise motivating his class that half the pupils are girls or that some of them come from very different cultural backgrounds. Only a very traditional teacher-centred kind of education can fail to take account of such facts.

More importantly, such an approach may underlie much of the no doubt quite unintentional systematic bias of the kind referred to earlier. For teachers to continue to 'teach their subject' in the traditional way without taking account of the differing interests and responses of different groups in the class is to teach in a way that will make one's subject less relevant and less approachable to some pupils than to others. Boys whose parents have recently arrived from Pakistan may not be able to identify with the struggles of King Alfred and the Danes quite as readily as their indigenous classmates. Likewise, mathematics teachers who pose their problems mainly in terms of men digging trenches or the trajectories of cricket balls, or only show an interest in pupils who shoot their hands up and compete for the teacher's attention, must take some of the responsibility for girls being 'turned off' their subject. It will be recalled that in the previous chapter we indicated that justice involves not only treating equals equally, but also treating relevantly different individuals differently. Someone committed to treating all his pupils fairly cannot therefore simply treat them all the same, particularly if this means continuing to treat all his pupils in the same way as he has been wont to treat one particular category of pupils in the past.

There is the further point that in the ethnic field 'treating them all the same' is essentially an assimilationist strategy (Bagley and Verma, 1983, pp. viii–xiii). The approach rather smacks of: 'I've nothing against blacks provided they behave themselves and conform to our standards; if they come to our country they must fall in with our ways, and not expect us to fall in with theirs' (cf. Willey, 1984, pp. 28–30). Yet there is no reason why someone who, for one reason or another, comes to live in Britain should be expected to give up his cultural identity or willingly see his children pressurized into doing so. There is equally no reason why, if they wish to gain acceptance at school, pupils whose parents have come from the Caribbean or from the Indian sub-continent should feel obliged to become invisible by abandoning their home language, their particular mode of dress, their own cultural interests or modes of relating to each other for the duration of the school day. The commitment to provide education for all cannot be conditional on such a concession.

MULTICULTURAL EDUCATION

In contrast to the view of groups of different races as a 'problem', to be resolved by assimilation into the indigenous monoculture, the official aim in Britain and elsewhere during the 1970s (Willey, 1984, pp. 24–5) came to be that of cultural pluralism. Official publications were inclined to assert that the country already possessed a multicultural society and that parents and pupils would hold a 'greater diversity of personal values' than previously. Ethnic groups, it was held, 'have a distinctive culture of their own' which 'should be sustained and other groups encouraged to recognize its authenticity'. Instead of the 'problem' of speakers of English as a second language it became the smart thing for heads to speak of their schools as being 'enriched' by the presence of varied ethnic backgrounds. Instead of playing down cultural diversity, schools favouring this approach attempt to introduce elements drawn from different cultures into the curriculum as well as into social and

111

other aspects of school life and some local authorites have gone some way to providing resources and back-up services to this end.

In many respects this approach seems very attractive in terms of educational aims. Here, apparently, is a way of providing a stimulating and varied programme. Children's understanding of other minds and other cultures is being developed and this in an authentic way by encouraging contact and interaction between different groups. Ethnocentricity would be combated and the moral values of tolerance and mutual respect encouraged.

Unfortunately, this has not always been the way things have worked out. Multicultural elements have tended to be grafted on to rather than integrated into the curriculum. They are often travestied beyond recognition even by the most committed teachers who are in no real position to understand them. They tend to be concentrated in low-status or marginal areas of the curriculum (music, the arts, general studies). They emphasize cultural differences rather than common humanity. In consequence, the members of minority groups may well come to be valued not as fully fledged participating members of mainstream society but as 'interesting', quaint or even bizarre. Doubt (Wilson, 1986) has even been expressed regarding the educational value of such 'multicultural' elements if they are chosen because they are supposed to be representative or characteristic, rather than because of their intrinsic excellence.

A more pressing objection is that such an approach baulks the fundamental issue of racism and inequality and may even be harmful by creating the impression that something important is being done, when it is not. Possibly members of other races may be glad to see their traditional ways survive and be understood, but they also have the right to achieve equality in the everyday life and mainstream educational programme of the country in which they are to live. Such considerations have led many educationists to urge that the 'multicultural' or 'pluralist' aims of the 1970s should be superseded by a more thoroughgoing form of anti-racist education.

ANTI-RACIST EDUCATION

It is important to begin by making the point that anti-racist education envisages no new, radical or particularly contentious set of aims. The aims remain those we have been considering all along, namely:

(1) Ensuring that children of all races and ethnic backgrounds are treated fairly while they are at school.
(2) Working for an adult society in which all individuals, irrespective of race or ethnic background, are treated justly and accorded equal respect.

The salient characteristic of anti-racist education lies, therefore, not in its aims but in the determination with which the above aims are pursued. It is an essential feature of anti-racist education that the problem of racism is recognized and tackled head on. What is sought is said to be a 'comprehensive interventionist approach to dismantling racism' (Willey, 1984, p. 93). The issue is 'firmly placed on the school agenda'. Characteristically, the whole school staff will discuss and attempt to work out a detailed policy for combating racism. This will normally include an unambiguous statement that all forms of racism are unacceptable. Staff are required to take seriously all forms of racial abuse or harassment, including racially derogatory jokes and remarks. A specific set of procedures may be given for dealing with such incidents, and these may entail the involvement of the head teacher or other very senior members of staff as well as the parents of the pupil concerned. It is also part of the policy of anti-racist education that, rather than attempting to graft multicultural elements on to the existing curriculum, the whole curriculum and indeed all parts of the school's work should be examined for racial bias. A thoroughgoing programme of anti-racist education might also include efforts to recruit and promote staff of ethnic minority origin and ensure proper representation of minority communities on the governing bodies.

By adopting specific procedures which may realistically be supposed to reduce the incidence of both deliberate and institutional racism in schools, and ultimately in society, schools may hope to communicate the message that their opposition is not mere lip-service, but is for real. The fact that these procedures may be costly in terms of effort and resources and may involve school authorities in confrontation with staff, pupils, parents and politicians is valuable in bringing home the seriousness of their commitment both to the perpetrators of racism and its victims.

What must, however, be constantly borne in mind is that the purpose of these procedures is not simply to promote the interests of certain ethnic groups, but to advance the larger and more fundamental aim of providing an education appropriate to a society

113

in which social justice is available to all. In this, ethnic minorities have common cause with other disadvantaged groups such as homosexuals, the handicapped, and the many members of the indigenous population who are economically underprivileged.

Possibly it makes political good sense to concentrate on what seem to be priorities, and pick off evils one by one. But arguably there would seem to be a case for adopting some of the more effective strategies of anti-racist education to combat all forms of social discrimination in so far as they are encouraged and perpetuated in and by the educational system.

PART IV

Intrinsic Values

Chapter Eleven

Liberal Education and Intrinsically Worthwhile Activities

In these final two chapters it is proposed to consider our third group of educational aims, namely those which are supposed to include in their justification notions of intrinsic value or the worthwhileness of pursuing certain kinds of knowledge, under-standing or activity for their own sakes. Though the successful pursuit of these aims will doubtless effect some kind of improve-ment in the learner, they are not primarily justified by being obviously in his interest, or because they develop something already present or inherent in him. They will doubtless broaden the scope of his autonomy and may well make him a more valuable employee. No doubt they will have valuable social side effects (Oakeshott, 1971, pp. 59–74) but these are incidental to or consequent on their supposed intrinsic value. For some writers (Peters, 1966, p. 85; Straughan and Wilson, 1983, pp. 16–33; Wilson and Cowell, 1983) these are the only truly educational aims, the political and social aims discussed in the previous four chapters being deprecatingly dismissed as regrettable concessions to political expediency.

Important among the aims, traditionally those of a liberal education, which are to be discussed in the present two chapters are commitment to and appreciation of certain artistic and cultural pursuits. The central place, however, is occupied by the intellectual activities involved in the pursuit of knowledge, understanding, truth and rationality.

Concern with aims of this kind frequently incurs the charge of elitism. For this there may appear to be some justification. Their

117

proponents (e.g. Cooper, 1980, pp. 53–62; O'Hear, 1981, pp. 15–19, 151–63) often stress the importance of a commitment to and appreciation of excellence. These aims are closely connected with the so-called 'high culture' and the subjects of the traditional curriculum. Concentration on 'the best that has been thought and said' is historically associated with the public schools and those that have sought to emulate them. Thus, according to one critical interpretation of liberal education and its aims, the disinterested study of literature, the arts, and other areas of human inquiry are simply the traditional leisure pursuits of the upper classes. Who else, after all, could afford to engage in disinterested study? These activities, so the interpretation goes, are naturally initiated by those who aspire to join the leisured elite. For Bourdieu and Passeron (1970) both arts and sciences but, above all, in the French context, the study of literature constitute the 'cultural arbitrary' of the dominant class, or rather of a particular fraction of that class. Those born into that class naturally possess familiarity with such things. Others who wish to enter must painfully and, for the most part, less successfully strive to acquire them through the educational system. In Britain the nineteenth-century nouveau riche sent his son to public school to be brought up 'as a gentleman', for further mobility could be impeded rather than helped by acquiring too close a knowledge of the useful trade that had been the basis of the father's wealth.

Today, of course, history, literature and many other subjects of the traditional curriculum are supposedly studied 'for their own sake'. Yet the overriding motive for many sixth form and higher education students is to get the good A-level grades or degree classes which are supposed to lead to better-paid jobs. Similarly at lower levels examination success, including success in the examination of subjects of no obvious utilitarian application, serve as our way of allocating people to different social and occupational categories. Success in these studies therefore appears to be sought above all as a means to higher earning power and social prestige. Here surely is proof, if proof were needed, that talk of intrinsically worthwhile activities pursued for their own sake is eyewash. Clearly pupils study English and history for much the same reasons as they study accountancy and electronics – to get on in the world. The only difference is that whereas accountancy and electronics may actually enable one to do something, an O-level, A-level, second-class degree or whatever in English literature or history serves students' material ambitions in a more general way, labelling them as a person of a certain social category, entitled to certain social expectations.

It is part of this argument, implied by Bourdieu's term 'cultural arbitrary', that the content of the subjects of the curriculum is of no value in itself, and might as well be collections of meaningless mumbo-jumbo which have to be memorized and regurgitated in a prescribed form in order to 'get one's ticket'. The attack by certain sociologists of knowledge on the notions of objectivity and truth (see various articles in Young, 1971) are often taken to entail just such an assertion. For if there are no objective standards of truth, value or whatever, decisions about what we are to teach become arbitrary. Talk of some activities being more worthwhile than others becomes at best vacuous and at worst part of a conspiracy to preserve and legitimate existing social distinctions.

This relativist position has been convincingly attacked by a number of writers (O'Hear, 1981, pp. 19–29; Bailey, 1984, pp. 192–225; Trigg, 1985, pp. 30–5), both connected and unconnected with education. In particular, it has been pointed out that there is an obvious inconsistency in asserting that nothing whatever can in any sense be objectively true and that all knowledge claims are necessarily invalid. For if this is the case, the claims of Young and his associates must themselves be arbitrary and invalid by the same token.

Other shortcomings in the relativist argument, notably the invalid inference from the fact that all bodies of knowledge are human constructs to the subjectivity of individual judgements once these bodies of knowledge are established, have also been effectively exposed (O'Hear, 1981, pp. 22–6).

It should be added that despite the elitist associations of liberal education and its traditional content, and despite the fact that some of its proponents have identified themselves with the political right, it is far from obvious that commitment to such values as knowledge, rationality, understanding and truth entails any such political orientation. On the contrary, in so far as an unjust distribution of wealth and power is made possible by ignorance and prejudice, the determined and single-minded pursuit of truth must ultimately prove more explosively radical than any amount of tendentious propaganda (Mardle, 1977).

If the disciplines of a liberal education are not to be explained away as some form of spurious social legitimation and do not have immediate practical usefulness, does their value lie in some more general utility they possess? This possibility is suggested by Bailey (1984, pp. 29–35), though he also goes on to argue that they are intrinsically valuable as well. According to such an interpretation, the disinterested pursuit of academic, literary and other cultural studies may not have immediate pay-off like the training of a spoke-fitter or lathe-operator, but it may enable the individual to join the occupational ladder at a higher point, and also confer upon him the understanding and other qualities that make it appropriate for him to do so.

This must not be mistaken for the old 'transfer of training' argument according to which practice in the rote learning of Latin declensions or lines of Shakespeare somehow fitted ex-public schoolboys to govern the Empire or master the complexities of Civil Service Regulations. For it is now generally accepted that 'practice' or 'training' in one area of learning does not automatically improve one's mental performance in others that are unrelated. The point is not to provide a tough intellectual education as a form of character building, as expressed in the view that 'it does not matter what a boy learns, so long as he heartily detests it'. Nor is our aim to accustom pupils to perform boring and meaningless tasks at school so that they are more willing to do so in later life.

As Bailey makes clear, a liberal education is not supposed to improve later performance in any such contingent way. The value of such studies lies in the particularly general and fundamental learnings they involve. In consequence, they will be relevant to many other things the individual will later wish to do or learn. As illustrations of learnings which may be more fundamental than others, Bailey suggests learning the principles of nutrition rather than particular recipes in home economics, and mathematical principles rather than individual formulae. In moral education, understanding the principle of considering the interests of others would be more fundamental than injunctions against scrumping apples. Fundamental learnings will not necessarily be elementary, for a grasp of the fundamentals of a subject may only come at a relatively advanced stage. It is nevertheless the purpose of much curriculum development work in many fields to identify the fundamentals of particular forms of understanding and find ways of presenting these to pupils in a form that is both accessible and intellectually reputable (Bruner, 1960, pp. 33–54) at as early a stage as possible.

Such 'fundamental' learning is therefore supposed to benefit pupils, not because it provides 'practice' or 'training' in the learning of difficult tasks, but because it logically forms part of later learnings of a less fundamental kind. Such learnings may be particularly relevant to those of an individual's judgements which do not depend on a single technical skill but on the rational appraisal of considerations drawn from a variety of fields. Such understanding is supposed to liberate from 'the present and the particular' and from blind concentration on a single aspect of a problem or situation. If valid, such an argument would give some support to the traditional demand that those occupying important managerial and administrative positions and whose actions may therefore affect the lives and interests of many people should have received a good general education, as well as having such technical expertise as their work may require.

Turning now specifically to arguments to the effect that certain activities are in some sense intrinsically as well as instrumentally worthwhile, it must be said that these are far from uncontroversial, and are sometimes obscure.

At this stage it may therefore be helpful to draw two distinctions, failure to observe which readily gives rise to confusion. These are the distinctions between:

(1) saying that something is *intrinsically* good (or worthwhile) and saying that it is *self-evidently* so; and
(2) saying that something is intrinsically good (or worthwhile) and saying that one does it for its own sake.

Intrinsically Good and Self-Evidently Good

One might have thought that this was a somewhat elementary and obvious distinction. Nevertheless, many seminar discussions appear to founder on the assumption that once something has been pronounced intrinsically worthwhile, no further justification is necessary or possible. This confusion is the result of a palpable slide from 'This is good in itself and not good because of some further good it will lead to' to 'If you cannot see why this is good, there are no further reasons I can give.'

Clearly there are many reasons for regarding something as good which do not at all relate to further goods that it will lead to. They relate to internal features of the object or activity being appraised. Of course, these reasons may themselves be challenged and the process of justification cannot go on for ever. Ultimately the chain of reasoning must seek to link back to assumptions which the challenger cannot consistently deny. All too frequently, however, the riposte 'If you cannot see . . .' is used, like the peremptory 'This is what we *mean* by education' (see above, p. 22), as a device for closing discussion. Needless to say, this often produces hostility and frustration in those who, failing to 'see' what they are supposed to see, are inclined to regard it as a version of the emperor's new clothes. In the present context we are not at all concerned with self-evidence, but with the intrinsically worthwhile, and with explicating as fully as possible reasons for believing that some activities have this characteristic while others do not.

Things Done for their Own Sake and Things Intrinsically Worthwhile

If we claim that an activity is intrinsically worthwhile our reasons must in some way be located in the activity, but the particular range of activities an individual engages in for their own sake will tell us as much about the individual as about the activities. To speak of these activities as being intrinsically worthwhile for a particular individual, as John White does (White, 1973, p. 17), fudges this distinction. White, of course, wishes to argue that no activities are especially worthwhile in themselves and that, except in special cases such as the drunkard who wishes to play with a dangerous weapon, decisions as to what is or is not worthwhile are ultimately subjective. His reason for wishing to see certain activities on the curriculum is to ensure that the individual genuinely has a full range of choices open to him in later life, and he does not imply that the curricular activities he specifies have anything about them which means that they ought to be particularly valued or enjoyed.

Now it is true that we do sometimes say that something may be valuable to some people, but not to others. A load of manure may be valuable to the farmer, but not to the owner of a riding stables, or a test-pilot. Momentoes of his old regiment may have value to the veteran, but not to others. Normally, however, the term 'valuable' makes more objective claims. The object so described not only is valued but, for one reason or another, ought to be valued. Maybe it is to be valued in utilitarian terms for what it can be exchanged for, but maybe it should be valued because it is in some way *worthy* to be valued. In this connection it is sometimes argued that for things to be good as a means, other things must be good as ends and it is commonly supposed that these other things must in some way be intrinsically good, or valuable in themselves. This is not quite right. For something to be good as a means it is only necessary that there should be other things which we want or do for their own sake, and there is certainly no lack of these. Among things people do for their own sake are eating and drinking (beyond the need to sustain life), playing dominoes and sun-bathing. Working to gain a small surplus income may be good as a means to be able to do some of these things.

There is not a great deal wrong with these activities but we should scarcely describe them as valuable or even worthwhile. Puritans might even urge us to do less of them and find something more worthwhile, or even more useful to do.

The things we do for their own sake, but certainly do not consider intrinsically valuable, include numerous trivial amusements. Significantly they would seem to include Mill's nineteenth-century example (Mill, 1861, p. 10) of the game of pushpin, for which more recent writers have thought it urbane to suggest numerous modern equivalents. Mill offers pushpin as a relatively valueless occupation which he contrasts with that of reading poetry.

Once we move into the realm of games, sports and pastimes, however, the position begins to change for frequently these involve some form of skill, judgement or other kind of human achievement. This may be some relatively low-level thing, such as flipping a ball into a hole, or tossing a hoop over a stake, or it may be something immensely challenging that requires years of practice, exquisite judgement and taste, or considerable skill and physical courage. Typically the participant is protected from too easily achieving the apparent object of the exercise by a set of rules or obstacles. Sand-bunkers are placed around the green in golf. Huntsmen do not shoot or poison the fox, which would certainly be quicker and cheaper than riding him down with horse and hounds, and crossing the Atlantic as a lone yachtswoman is less obviously efficient than flying by Concorde. The true object of the exercise, that which makes it 'worthwhile', is not filling the hole with balls, pest-control, or arriving in New York but the exercise of skill, judgement, courage and so on which takes place as part of the process.

According to a view which has been influential in the philosophy of education, many human activities are capable of being carried on in this disinterested spirit, in which the participant's eye is fixed less on the utilitarian outcome than upon the inherent standards or excellences the activity entails. The craftsman may take as much pride in his craftmanship as in the sale-price of his artefact, the businessman may take satisfaction in the running of an efficient and enterprising business over and above that derived from the profit he receives, and the politician may be genuinely moved by the ideal he pursues, quite apart from any personal advantage he may gain when his party comes to power.

In the case of our most valued cultural and intellectual activities, however, the aspect of disinterested attachment to the inherent standards of the activity becomes paramount. Artists are not supposed to compromise their art for the sake of lucrative popularity; scientists and philosophers are not supposed to bend the evidence or fudge the argument for the sake of political expediency or social approval, even when this would be advantageous to themselves or their institution.

The final twist to the story is provided by the fact that many of our most highly esteemed activities, and those which are often regarded as central to the educational curriculum, are intellectual activities. Besides being challenging, involving standards and being essentially disinterested, they involve the pursuit of truth and the rational criticism and appraisal of claims to truth in various areas. This is supposed to lead to a particular, so-called 'transcendental' line of justification. This rests upon the fact that there appears to be some inconsistency in seeking to know what activities one should value or engage in while disvaluing just those forms of rational inquiry that might enable one to find out.

In claiming that certain disinterested pursuits are more worthwhile than many other activities it may be relevant to point out (cf. Mill, 1861, p. 8) that as a matter of fact they are valued, especially by the more successful and fortunate members of our society who have most choice about how they and their dependents will spend their time. The argument is not a strong one, however, for there are many rich philistines. Also, the reasons why they are chosen may have little to do with their actual value. Fashion and social prestige will certainly play a part in many cases (Arnold, 1869, p. 43), as, no doubt, will psychological factors. Maslow (1954), for example, argues that when such basic drives as the need for food and security have been satisfied the behaviour of human beings is controlled by more sophisticated drives for mastery, self-actualization and self-esteem. This might be one reason why some individuals prefer Griffith's activities (Griffiths, 1965, p. 190) which are 'interesting', 'absorbing', 'fascinating', 'varied', 'unpredictable in detail and requiring constant adjustment and the exercise of new modes of action'. That some people prefer such activities is therefore no conclusive reason for supposing that they are inherently valuable. Some people may just happen to be made that way. Others clearly are not.

That an activity satisfies the need for self-esteem is also no reason for supposing that it necessarily is estimable or objectively worthwhile in any way. For something to meet the need for self-esteem it is only necessary that it should be thought admirable by the individual and his society.

More cogent as an argument to show that the standards inherent in many activities are non-arbitrary and contribute something to the value of that activity is the following. To do something well is to do what anyone who engages in the activity, however badly, must be trying to do. To take a banal example, to play golf, however badly, is to try to get the ball into the hole in as few shots as possible. There is no other way of playing golf. The top professional just does what everyone else would do if they could. Of course, we can ask, 'Why play golf at all?' but the general point remains that to attempt to engage in any physical activity is to be committed to doing it as skilfully as one can, and to accept that someone who does it more skilfully is doing it better. Within activities that define and are defined by their internal standards, there can be no room for relativism.

Likewise, anyone who attempts to sing at all must be attempting to do so melodiously and harmoniously. The rawest newcomer to the business of pottery must hope that his vessel will be of pleasing appearance and watertight, and anyone who attempts to investigate the nature of the physical world necessarily makes statements that he hopes will withstand the test of evidence. Of course, as the beginner progresses towards supreme expertise he may be solicited by more sophisticated interpretations of the notions of musicality, aesthetic appearance and valid evidence, and simplistic

125

notions may be rejected as banal or commonplace. Substantially, however, the ideal, that is the standard, remains the same even though it is no longer within the comprehension of the novice. For the educator, this is reassuring. It means that both he and his pupils may genuinely fall short of what they should be aiming for. But it also means that there is some point in attempting to correct their efforts. He is not, as relativists claim, necessarily imposing arbitrary demands upon them. It is also the case that the attempts of his newest and least talented pupil have some value if, that is, the performance of the masters of the activity has any. When the child begins to sing or paint or describe the world, there is no hypocrisy in praising his effort, and no act of deception is involved in constructive criticism or encouragement to improve.

This point also helps us to understand why educators set so much value upon excellence. The standards of achievement involved are those which we are bound to value if we value or engage in the activity at all. If we value them in everyday performances, then logically we must set a correspondingly higher value on performances in which they are superlatively achieved.

Needless to say, the fact that we set a high value on excellence does not mean that we would regard it as a reason for setting aside other, for example, moral values, or other legitimate educational aims. White quite properly criticizes unbalanced educational programmes which may cause misery to the child and hamper his all-round development in the pursuit of some particular form of artistic or academic excellence (White, 1982, pp. 16–17). We may also feel justified in rejecting blatantly unfair distributions of educational resources in the name of excellence, when this is simply a pretext for favouring children from a particular social stratum.

Moving to another aspect of intrinsically worthwhile activities White suggests that we cannot know in advance in the case of a particular child what 'kinds of activities or ways of life (will) be intrinsically valuable for him later to pursue' (White, 1973, p. 17) and criticizes an educational approach which presents certain cultural pursuits in such a way that people feel morally guilty if they do not engage in them.

In the end, no doubt, one must agree with White on both of these points. There are, however, certain distinctions to be made if they are not to be misunderstood.

It is certainly true that we cannot know in advance what an

individual will become committed to or engage in later on. This will partly depend on such things as temperament, ability and leisure opportunities as well as on the tastes and inclinations of others with whom he lives in close proximity. To present certain activities to him as uniquely valuable is therefore unjustifiable and unkind and risks leaving him feeling inadequate, both in the present and in later life. Certain cultural and intellectual activities have, however, afforded many individuals considerable satisfaction and enrichment and are presumably capable of doing the same for at least some of our pupils. In an undiluted form they may be somewhat inaccessible to the uninitiate, particularly in the case of pupils who receive no introduction to them from their home background. Clearly, if pupils are to engage in these activities they must receive some initiation into them, not as something one ought to enjoy on pain of being thought coarse and uncivilized, but as something which may be enjoyed and valued, and ought to be given a chance.

Closely connected with this is the fact that the notion of disinterested commitment in general is an important part of someone's moral and personal education. Of course, individuals must be committed to truth-telling, fairness, and consideration for others, even when these things bring about no obvious benefit to themselves. But it is also important for the individual to come to value at least *some* activities and pursuits for their own sake. These activities may include an individual's work. Even in relatively lucrative occupations many people have a commitment to the work they do over and above the income they derive from it. But people may be committed to other things as well. These may be the traditional 'high culture' pursuits, but may equally include many other less high-faluting occupations and pastimes.

In addition to games lessons many schools offer a range of extra-curricular activities, clubs and so on. These tend to be explained as either useful for the sake of physical fitness or valuable for some other reason such as developing character or team spirit, promoting good informal relations between staff and pupils, creating a good public image, or whatever. Or they may be dismissed as peripheral amusements by those unsympathetic to education.

Learning to do things because one wants to do them, or because one likes doing them, may be a very proper and not unimportant part of the child's upbringing. Just what things they are may not matter provided they are reputable, and have sufficient in them to prove engaging over a period. The only essential thing is that they should not be seen and presented to pupils as some form of extra qualification to be added to university or employment profiles. To grow up without this capacity for absorption in things to some extent for their own sake is to face the prospect of an unsatisfying, impoverished sort of life.

Such a person is effectively a slave. If nothing he does serves ends of his own, he ultimately serves only the ends of others. He can be more or less precisely controlled by manipulating the environment of reward and disadvantage. He may be sent scurrying from occupation to occupation, or from one end of the country to the other by simple changes in wage or salary structures. He is biddable, corruptible and expendable, for valuing nothing but what is useful, his own value lies only in his usefulness. It is perhaps not surprising that authoritarian governments and institutions are suspicious of multiple commitments, particularly to things and activities of intrinsic value.

In his keenness to make the point that there are no activities to which everyone is necessarily obliged to be committed, White fails to make a second distinction between being committed to actually engage in an activity and seeing, understanding and appreciating what there is to value or admire in it. Which activities we actually decide to engage in will naturally vary from individual to individual as a result of temperament and other things. Within limits this choice is up to us. Maybe, as White implies, there is no irrationality in rejecting what others have found fascinating or absorbing. But what is admirable we are bound to admire, whatever our temperament or circumstances.

I am not committed to engage in mountaineering and I am sure there is no reason why I should be. But it would be mean-minded of me to dismiss the climbing of Everest as 'simply a waste of time and effort'. The achievement involves planning, courage, judgement, skill and so on of the highest order, and admiration and applause are the only appropriate responses. Needless to say, the same applies in the case of cultural artistic and intellectual activities. Ignorant rejection is particularly likely in these areas because of the outwardly unspectacular nature of achievement in many of them, and the difficulty of understanding the criteria of excellence involved. Such rejection may also be a perfectly understandable reaction to the contempt sometimes shown by those who understand these things towards those who do not.

White's strictures against indoctrination and unjustifiable constraint may well be valid against attempts to get pupils committed to certain specific activities, in the sense of actually feeling obliged to engage in them. They are not, however, valid objections to the claim that pupils should come to value such activities, in the sense of seeing what there is in them to value and admire. Possibly this distinction will go some way towards explaining Peters's hesitation (1973c, p. 250) regarding Plato's claim that to understand the good is to be committed to it. To understand the good certainly involves seeing why it is good and why it is to be valued. It would be surprising if, having seen what there is in an activity to be admired, many individuals did not feel also drawn to try their own hand at it. But whether they in fact do so may depend on contingent factors such as opportunity and inclination.

On the third point, no doubt White (1973, p. 16) is right to fear that pupils will confuse the suggestion that they really ought to read *War and Peace* or attend symphony concerts with the oughts of moral obligation. This, however, is a confusion which needs to be sorted out, rather than shied away from. The adult who derives from the reading of *War and Peace* the delight or fascination that White claims to derive from it will naturally wish to share it with others. Why not? It may enrich them, without impoverishing us. But clearly there can be no obligation to enjoy it – and to read on without enjoyment is pointless. It benefits nobody.

Possibly some irrationality is involved in neglecting the opportunity to extend one's knowledge or develop one's talents. But life is short and one has many things to attend to. The development of a talent is to be praised and admired, not approved or condemned. It is subject to critical rather than moral appraisal. If it is still thought that the individual has some kind of duty to improve himself (and to develop one's talents undoubtedly is to improve oneself) this is at most a duty of imperfect of obligation. Though in general we ought to do these things, since we benefit from the talents of others, the individual has latitude in the choice of mode and occasion, for no one suffers unmerited harm as the result of any particular omission.

In this chapter we have begun our consideration of the view that one important group of educational aims is concerned with introducing pupils to certain activities which are in some way intrinsically worthwhile. As a preface to this we considered and

129

rejected the relativist view that notions of truth and value are necessarily spurious, and that the subjects of the school curriculum simply serve the purposes of social differentiation. We also examined sympathetically the view that sustained and disinterested study of these subjects may be of general utility.

It was argued that if certain activities are of intrinsic value, this derives from the internal standards definitive of the activities in question. In coming to understand and appreciate such activities, it was suggested, the rational response is critical approval and admiration rather than any moral obligation to engage in them ourselves. Whether or not we do so will depend on psychological and other facts about us.

For the most part, our remarks to date have been applicable to a wide range of activities which may be performed well or less well depending on the competence and commitment of the performer. In the course of this chapter we have made reference to specifically intellectual activities which constitute a sub-group within the general category of activities which are held to be intrinsically worthwhile. In so doing we touched only briefly upon the possibility that these activities may be subject to an additional line of justification deriving from the nature of rationality and rational inquiry. This line of justification will be explored in detail in our final chapter.

Chapter Twelve

The Centrality of the Cognitive

Over and above the features of worthwhile activities in general, intellectual activities are held to possess a number of further attractive characteristics. For some people, at least, they are intensely absorbing if not always pleasurable (Elliott, 1977). They are held to be unending in scope, serious and, though capable of generating intense rivalries, essentially non-competitive in respect of their objects. One may make discoveries in science or originate new arguments in philosophy without depriving others of the opportunity of doing the same. They are challenging and provide opportunities for a variety of excellences in seemingly limitless gradations of perfection. They entail both standards appropriate to the particular disciplines and the exercise of certain general intellectual virtues such as intelligence, persistence, integrity, clarity, respect for evidence, and non-arbitrariness. By contrast with sports and games, which may certainly be intrinsically worthwhile in their way, intellectual pursuits have the additional quality of being 'serious' and of throwing light on other important aspects of the individual's life and situation.

In addition, intellectual pursuits are held to benefit from a further mode of justification by virtue of their connection with knowledge and rationality. It is convenient to begin our examination of this view with a consideration of two of the earliest and most widely quoted versions of it.

According to Peters (1966, pp. 166–66), if one seriously poses the question, 'Why do this rather than that?' one is committed to considering anything which may throw light upon the answer. The various kinds of intellectual inquiry available may all, so Peters argues, throw light on the answer to this question and, furthermore, what they have to say cannot be understood unless one actually engages in those inquiries to some extent. Even to ask this question seriously, he claims, entails a commitment to engage in inquiries of this kind.

With Hirst (1965), the emphasis is somewhat different, though in its fundamentals the argument is essentially the same. The main thrust of the article in which it appears is to develop the author's claim that there are various kinds or forms of knowledge, each distinguished by its subject matter, its central concepts, logical structure, characteristic modes of investigation and tests for truth or validity. The grasp of these forms of knowledge or modes of experience is constitutive of the development of mind itself. To ask for justification of this process only makes sense if one is already seeking valid knowledge, that is, knowledge as to how this process is to be justified. Though one can ask for the justification of particular activities, Hirst claims, one cannot reasonably ask for justification of the process of justification itself. All forms of knowledge, furthermore, contribute to our moral understanding; to our understanding of what we should do and how we should live.

It should be noted that in both versions of the argument there are two points of emphasis, largely independent of each other. First, there is the claim that there would be some illogicality or contradiction in supposing that someone can seriously ask what one should do, or why one should engage in certain activities, while doubting that he is already committed to the pursuit of serious inquiries. Secondly, there is the claim that the various forms of intellectual inquiry throw light on the question of what an individual ought to do or how he ought to conduct his life. It is of importance to distinguish between these two aspects of the argument, since a frequently heard and possibly valid objection relates only to the first of these and does not touch the second.

White (1982, pp. 10–14), among others, deals somewhat dismissively with the first part of the argument. He claims that to ask 'Should I pursue knowledge?' may commit one to a concern with truth, but only in respect of that particular question. It does not commit one to any wider range of intellectual inquiry any more than does asking someone the time. If we have in the past rather

132

readily accepted the view that the pursuit of knowledge is self-justifying, this, White claims, is on account of other theories which we no longer find acceptable. In particular, he points to Hegelian Idealism according to which God, as Mind, is immanent in Nature and seeks to realize Himself through the extension of human consciousness, and Dewey's evolutionary ethics in which the growth of human learning in the form of problem-solving has a critical part to play in the advance of the human race.

White's tracing of this part of the history of educational ideas is fascinating and entirely convincing. As White himself would be the first to stress, however, the fact that a view has at some time drawn support from an invalid theory does not prove it to be false even though, as the result of a kind of guilt by association, it may be discredited in the eyes of a reader. The part of the argument here under discussion, however, deserves to be rejected for a number of other reasons.

There is about it a rather circular *ad hominem* quality. A possible objector is effectively slapped down by being made to seem as if he has asked a nonsensical question, but no positive reasons are provided for thinking that intellectual activities ought to be valued. The all important question: 'So why ought these activities to be pursued, then?' is simply ruled out of court. Even if it is true, as Hirst says (1965, pp. 126–7), that a certain contradiction is involved in asking for justification of the process of justification itself, our question ultimately remains unanswered and we are left unsatisfied and perplexed. The person who asks for justification may already be committed to the process of justification, but it is not clear from this why anyone else should be. Yet, despite this, Hirst and more especially Peters happily, and in my view perfectly satisfactorily, provide justification for the pursuit of intellectual activities in the other part of their argument.

White's objection and the disparaging remarks of those who follow him (see e.g. Bailey, 1984, p. 38) seem to ignore the full amplitude of Peter's argument. It is certainly true that anyone who asks a question normally manifests an interest in the truth regarding the answer to that specific question, and not much else. But very general questions such as those regarding the nature of the good life, or what activities someone ought to commit himself to are of a rather special kind, a point disguised by the more restricted question, 'Why pursue knowledge?' which White (1982, p. 10) examines. The point, as Peters spells out very clearly (1966,

p. 161; 1973c, pp. 258–262), is that we cannot satisfactorily answer such profound questions without a good deal of knowledge and sustained reflection. One needs, for example, to know a great deal about the world and what it contains, about human affairs and the way they are arranged, about oneself and the human condition, about values and their justification and (if such there be) about the supernatural context of human life. Anyone who is seriously concerned to discover the nature of the good life – which cannot be stated simply like the answer to the man who asks the time – will be interested in the researches and reflections both of his contemporaries, and those who have lived before him.

But precisely these are the bodies of inquiry and reflection which constitute the great disciplines of the human mind, our 'forms of knowledge', or 'modes of experience'. They cannot be fully understood without engaging in them. Yet serious reflection on such things is essential to the 'examined life' which is alone worth living, for it alone is freely lived in accordance with valid reasons rather than habit, tradition, blind unconcern or the demands of others.

It might be thought that this kind of argument for intellectual pursuits is an instrumental one. The argument appears to be saying that we study various forms of knowledge and so on in order to know what way of life to choose, in much the same way that a farmer might consult his supplier's catalogue in order to find out what poison to use to get rid of the rats in his barn. Peters (1973c, p. 258) attempts to show why this view is mistaken by contrasting the action of keeping fit (in order not to make the choice in a sluggish or slovenly way) with pursuing a wide range of intellectual inquiries which will enable us to choose wisely. According to Peters, the difference lies in the fact that being reasonably fit is simply an empirically necessary condition and hence is properly regarded as instrumental. Whereas the processes of choice and justification are linked to knowledge and understanding by such logical relationships as 'relevance', 'providing evidence', 'illuminating' and 'explaining'.

Coming to see what is involved in choosing a certain way of life is an integral part of the process of choosing whether to pursue it or not. If we are committed to making such profound choices in life, as it will be argued we are, there is logically no way we can willingly avoid considering such things as are relevant to this choice. By contrast, the need to be physically fit in order to decide properly –

if this were indeed necessary – would simply be the result of the particular make-up of the human organism.

Needing to know which rat-poison to use is contingent in a rather different way. The need to know this depends on the prior decision that the rats need to be got rid of, and this may depend on a number of further considerations. The need to choose one's way of life is inescapable and all have an interest in choosing wisely.

It is also necessary to take account of a number of reservations which may be felt, especially by those involved in the everyday business of teaching across the whole range of ability and academic aspiration.

To begin with, the justification given above only seems to operate among philosophers. On the argument so far, the only person who seems to be committed to engaging in a range of intellectual pursuits would seem to be the sort of person who actually asks 'What should I be doing with my life?' or whatever. It would never occur to many human beings ever to formulate this question. The Greek gentleman farmer or leisured eighteenth-century aristocrat might be tortured by the problem of how to occupy his time, but for most people the problem is finding time to do the things we know we have to do. To the hard-pressed house-person (or her husband) the appropriate response to the question 'What should I do with my life?' might seem to be 'I wish I had your problems'. It might indeed even be asked whether people have any choice about the lives they lead, or whether the suggestion that they have is not simply an ideological device to conceal the truly coercive conditions under which most people live. This, however, would be to take an unduly literal view of things. Unlike those of animals and other creatures, our lives are not governed by a range of automatic responses and genetically programmed behaviour patterns or, at least, not entirely so. Much of our behaviour is to be explained not in terms of stimulus and response, but of social institutions, practices, approved standards of behaviour and the significance or appraisal we attach to someone's behaving thus and not otherwise (Oakeshott, 1971, pp. 43–7). Even when our behaviour is at its most conventional it is usually the case that we could, if we chose, act differently. To this extent human beings are, like it or not, irremediably free and consequently 'subject to the demands of reason' (Peters, 1973c, p. 254). It is always possible to ask 'Is this what I want or ought to be doing?' 'For what reason?' 'Is that reason sound?' and so on. Even

135

those who never think of asking these questions could in principle always do so.

In fact, the suggestion that choice only occurs in rather elite social contexts is rather patronizing. We all know that questions such as 'Do I really want to be doing this, living like this?' come up pretty frequently in our own lives, even though we may hurriedly busy ourselves with something more immediately practical in order to brush them aside. In Western society, even in times of limited employment opportunities, vocational choices face most people at some point, especially in the later stages of their formal education. We do not, of course, choose our occupation freely, for our choice is limited by the options available. But even those who feel they must take whatever opportunities turn up usually have some clear idea of things they will not do in order to earn a living. Some occupations will be too disagreeable, degrading or disreputable.

Apart from the vocational area, the individual also has a range of options in the matter of life-style, how he will relate to others, and which others he will relate to. He will also make more or less conscious decisions regarding his spending priorities, leisure pursuits and the degree of his commitment to the various activities he engages in.

It may be thought that in more primitive communities the range of options open to the individual is more restricted than in even the most deprived Western milieu. Consequently, it might seem that the cognitive and speculative activities of the kind we have been discussing are something of a Western idiosyncrasy of little importance to the great mass of humanity that inhabit the huts and villages across the world. Significantly, however, all societies seem to possess a web of beliefs and appraisals which give meaning to what the group does and prescribes how life should be lived. It would, indeed, be difficult to conceive of a society in which this were not true.

Two things are to be said about this fact. The first is that though these systems of belief and appraisal prescribe how life should be lived, they do not determine it. The tribesman or peasant may have no possibility of becoming a ballet dancer or engine driver. Even his place within his group may be closely circumscribed. But even within the local value system he may be a more or a less brave warrior or hunter, a more or a less reverent performer of the rituals, a more or a less careful tiller of the soil, and so on. Within the group, some will be more conformist than others and no doubt there will be grumblers, recalcitrants, rebels and rank outsiders.

The second thing to be said is that if there is a system of beliefs that governs one's behaviour, everyone has the strongest possible interest in knowing whether those beliefs are true. The belief may relate to the best ways of producing healthy crops, the sinfulness of taking a more varied diet, the prospects of a satisfactory life in the township over the hill, or the dire punishment that awaits adulterers in the after-life. If the local beliefs in these matters are false, one wants to know in order to arrange one's affairs most advantageously. In both advanced and more primitive societies, the individual has but one life and misinformation or a failure to appreciate the true nature of the options open to one and the consequences of one's choices may prove costly.

The various forms of intellectual inquiry we possess, with their tests for truth and procedures of criticism and appraisal, are, of course, designed to liberate people from beliefs that are limited or untenable – Bacon's idols of the tribe, den, cave and market place.

This is no arrogant assertion of the primacy of any particular 'Western' form of rationality. As will have been clear, the point is that all human beings have an interest in scrutinizing their beliefs with whatever are the best means available to them. One might think that recently evolved Western intellectual approaches, with their rejection of authority, built-in procedures to allow for openness and change and insistence on public standards of evidence and argument have certain advantages, including a powerful unifying function in an increasingly inter-communicating world. But experience and more open-minded attention to other traditions may eventually suggest that our understandings are shallow, lacking in subtlety or deficient in ways we have not yet learnt to appreciate. There can be no final count of ways of apprehending the world and the individual's position in it. Consequently, there can be no final answer to the question, 'How should one live one's life?', or even 'What considerations are relevant to the answering of this question?'

This stress upon the importance of the cognitive for all human beings is particularly necessary in view of recent suggestion that, for some citizens at least, an education centrally based on knowledge and understanding may be inappropriate (Bantock, 1968; FEU, 1979). Narrow interpretations of the recent slogan 'Education for Capability' (Burgess, 1986, p. ix) may also encourage such tendencies. But, as may have been inferred from previous paragraphs, if pupils are not given access to knowledge and understanding – real knowledge and understanding, that is – which actually enables them to comprehend and to a degree control their own lives, they will acquire something else instead. Groups may generate their own folk wisdom, their own explanations of the way things are, their own maxims of prudent or admirable conduct.

Willis (1977) graphically shows this process in action among working-class adolescents turned off by the formal educational system. Whatever advantages in terms of relevance and accessibility may be claimed for such 'knowledge' generated by the group in the light of its own life needs, however, it is bound to have grave shortcomings. Without the rigorous testing and scrutiny from which mainstream knowledge profits, it will be more parochial, more limited, more prone to prejudice and error and, above all, calculated to anaesthetize rather than to liberate. This is always supposing, of course, that those for whom 'an intellectual education is not appropriate' are not simply fed a set of attitudes and commitments which it suits the interest of others for them to adopt.

In suggesting that the promotion of knowledge and understanding should be regarded as centrally important educational aims, it is not assumed that old-fashioned, so-called 'didactic' teaching methods said to be typical of 'academic' schools in the past are the best way of developing the cognitive abilities of all, or indeed any, pupils. Rightly used it seems quite likely that newer, apparently more practical methods involving group discussion in which pupils are brought to grasp the point and purpose of their own learning will be more effective in this regard. But such approaches need not only careful monitoring but a clear understanding on the part of the teacher that the aim remains that of cognitive development rather than mere performance or the exercise of social or communication skills.

Knowledge and understanding are not, of course, the only things children must acquire during their upbringing. Not only must individuals comprehend and, as far as possible, choose the life they are to lead, they must also be capable of meeting its demands. This may well entail acquiring certain vocational skills at an appropriate point. One not only needs the ability to make discriminations of value but also the moral character to act accordingly. One needs a sensitive understanding of others, but also the interpersonal competence to manage one's relations with them successfully. One needs to understand the workings of society and its faults, but also the abilities and commitment to do something about them.

All citizens, like the teachers who are drawn from their ranks, need both knowledge and understanding to choose and to reflect upon their aims, and also the skills and capabilities to carry them out. But the practical and the cognitive are not two equal and balancing educational requirements. Skills and competences, unlike knacks, dodges, reflexes and instinctive behaviours are inconceivable without a good deal of knowledge and understanding. Quite apart from this, however, a world peopled by individuals with a high degree of capability, skill, persistence and so on but insufficiently guided by judgement, reflection and criticism would be a veritable nightmare. Such individuals, whether teachers or citizens in general, are potential juggernauts.

For this reason, the education of both teachers and citizens must, in its aims if not always in its methods, retain a central and fundamental bias towards the cognitive.

Suggestions for Further Reading

Chapter 1

A central text for the understanding of an aim and its relationship to the activity to which it belongs is Peters (1964). Dewey (1916, pp. 100–10) also throws valuable light on the question, and the issue is taken further by Peters (1973b; 1973e) and by Sockett (1972). Davies (1976) provides a sound and thorough account of the contrasting notion of an objective, including a behavioural objective.

Chapter 2

Peters (1964, 1973b) and Hirst and Peters (1970, pp. 1–41) discuss the concept of education at length. White (1970) is widely regarded as the standard piece on indoctrination. Degenhardt (1976) adopts a similar point of view and Snook (1972) is a useful collection of articles on the subject. White (1972) explores the relationship between education and socialization.

Those who wish to follow up traditional theories of ethics are referred to Raphael (1981), Warnock (1967), MacIntyre (1967) and Williams (1972), and for a brief summary of the main theories, Peters (1966, ch. 3).

Scheffler (1962, pp. 11–35) deals with attempts to derive imperatives from definitions (of education) but serious students may wish to consult the classical source of his argument in Hume (1751, 3.I.i, pp. 507–20) as well as work on essentially contested concepts by Montefiore (1979) and Naish (1984). A discussion of the relationship between individual and social aims is to be found in Hargreaves (1982) who argues for giving greater attention to the latter, and valuable light is thrown on the historical development of this relationship, as well as on that between individual and social aims and the pursuit of knowledge and reason, in White (1978), White and Gordon (1979) and White (1982, pp. 9–22).

This last mentioned work as a whole is essential reading for anyone concerned with the philosophy of educational aims.

Further Reading

Chapter 3

The best-known exponent of utilitarianism in an educational context is Barrow (1975a; 1975b; 1976). Wilson (1979, pp. 135–62) and especially Dearden (1972c) may also be consulted with profit. Mill (1861) is an accessible primary source for the doctrine of utilitarianism of which Smart and Williams (1973) is a full but readable critique. The general works on ethics mentioned above also have very satisfactory sections on utilitarianism.

Chapter 4

For discussion of the 'child-centred' aims of 'growth' and meeting the needs and interests of the child see Dearden (1972a; 1972b), Peters (1969) and Wilson (1971).

Those wishing to pursue the topic of child-centred education in a wider historical context are referred to Rousseau (1726b), Dewey (1938), Neill (1962) and Montessori (1936) in the first instance.

Chapter 5

The most lucid and satisfactory treatment of autonomy is Dearden (1975), but see also Dearden (1972d), Gewirth (1973) and, for a slightly different perspective, Crittenden (1978). Bonnett (1986) tackles the subject of authenticity but the essential text on this topic is Cooper (1983).

Those wishing to pursue the implications of existentialism may find Sartre (1946) and Warnock (1967) reasonable starting points. By far the most accessible and convincing expressions of the existentialist value of authenticity, however, are to be found in literary rather than academic works. Sartre's *Les Mains Sales*, Anouilh's *Antigone* and Camus's *L'Etranger* are all highly readable and available in English translation. Sartre's *La Nausée* is frequently quoted as a key source but is usually reckoned to be heavier going.

Chapter 6

This chapter draws heavily on material and argument included in Wringe (1981a). Relevant additional reading falls into three main categories. Useful references to official and quasi official statements of policy are to be found in Wringe (1981a) and Bailey (1984, ch. 9). The bibliography of Rees and Atkinson (1982) contains details of MSC publications. Secondly, there are radical critiques of vocational schemes and policies. Rees and Atkinson

(1982) and Gleeson (1983) adequately convey the flavour of these. Thirdly, a relatively small number of philosophical treatments exist of the issues involved. Bailey (1984, ch. 9) is scholarly and thorough and Jonathan (1983) provides a stimulating and rigorous treatment of a number of important aspects, particularly the notion of generic skills. See Dewey (1916, ch. 23) for an earlier treatment of the central issue.

Chapter 7

Straughan (1982) provides an excellent introduction to the subject of moral education, with many useful references and suggestions for further reading. Other widely used introductory accounts are Wilson, Williams and Sugarman (1967) and Downey and Kelly (1978). For further reading on socialization and indoctrination see suggestions for Chapter 2 above: White (1972), White (1970), Degenhardt (1976) and Snook (1972).

Chapter 8

Anyone seriously interested in the issues of equality and social justice will wish to be acquainted with some of the major texts of the Enlightenment on this subject such as Rousseau (1762a), Paine (1791) and especially Locke (1689–90, Second Treatise).

For a variety of perspectives on the twentieth-century debate on equality of opportunity in education see Crosland (1962), Jencks (1975) and Cooper (1980).

Chapter 9

Nozick (1974) and Rawls (1973) are discussed in this chapter and though these (especially the latter) are substantial works, many readers will no doubt wish to consult the originals. The essential chapter for Nozick's concept of justice is Chapter 7. The main outlines of Rawls's position are developed in Part I. Barry (1965) provides a useful critical commentary on Rawls.

Peters (1966, ch. 4) and even Benn and Peters (1959, ch. 5) may usefully be consulted for accounts of the older concept of justice as fairness.

Chapter 10

There exists a good deal of material detailing the mechanisms which lead to inequality and injustice in respect of race and gender, and make positive recommendations for policy. Philosophical treatments of both issues are rare. In this regard Richards (1980) is a must on gender and Mill (1883) provides an earlier philosophical treatment of the topic.

Arnot (1985) brings together a collection of stimulating articles on both race and gender. Philosophical issues related to cultural pluralism in education are discussed by Zec (1980) and Wilson (1986). The 900-page Swann Report (Department of Education and Science, 1985), or a summary of its main findings, will be necessary reading for anyone concerned with this issue.

Willey (1984) is a good introductory account of alternative responses to the racial situation in schools and Bagley and Verma (1983) is a collection of studies of the experience of ethnic minority children and adolescents in Britain.

Goldman (1979) and Dworkin (1977, pp. 223–39) discuss in detail issues raised by the practice of reverse discrimination.

Chapters 11 and 12

In the literature of the philosophy of education there is no shortage of material on the issues discussed in these two chapters. Peters (1966, ch. 5), Hirst (1965) and Peters (1937c), as well as Elliott (1975), are central, but additional and more critical accounts are provided by White (1973, pp. 5–24; 1982, pp. 9–22), Barrow (1976, ch. 3), Degenhardt (1982) and Bailey (1984). A reading of Winch (1958) and Oakeshott (1971) is valuable for their emphasis on the part played by the cognitive in human affairs. A wider perspective on rationality is provided by the various essays (especially that by Lukes) in Wilson (1974). For an outright rejection of the view presented in these chapters, see various articles (notably those by Esland and by Young himself) in Young (1971). In this connection see also Bourdieu and Passeron (1970) which is, however, not easy reading in either English or French.

Bibliography

Althusser, L. (1972) 'Ideology and ideological state apparatuses' in Cosin (1972), pp. 242–80.

Archambault, R. D. (1965), *Philosophical Analysis and Education* (London: Routledge & Kegan Paul).

Arnold, M. (1869), *Culture and Anarchy* (Cambridge: Cambridge University Press, 1960).

Arnot, M. (1985), *Race and Gender* (Oxford: Pergamon).

Bagley, C. and Verma, G. K. (eds) (1983), *Multicultural Childhood* (Aldershot: Gower).

Bailey, C. (1984), *Beyond the Present and the Particular* (London: Routledge & Kegan Paul).

Bantock, G. H. (1968), *Culture, Industrialisation and Education* (London: Routledge & Kegan Paul).

Barrow, R. (1975a), *Moral Philosophy for Eduation* (London: Allen & Unwin).

Barrow, R. (1975b), *Plato, Utilitarianism and Eduation* (London: Routledge & Kegan Paul).

Barrow, R. (1976), *Commonsense and the Curriculum* (London: Allen & Unwin).

Barry, B. (1965), *Political Argument* (London: Routledge & Kegan Paul).

Barry, B. (1973), *The Liberal Theory of Justice* (Oxford: Clarendon Press).

Benjamin, H. (1939), 'The Saber-tooth curriculum', in Hooper (1971), pp. 7–15).

Benn, S. I. and Peters, R. S. (1959), *Social Principles and the Democratic State* (London: Allen & Unwin).

Bennett, N. (1976), *Teaching Styles and Pupil Progress* (London: Open Books).

Bereiter, C. (1973), *Must We Educate?* (Englewood Cliffs, NJ: Prentice-Hall).

Berlin, I. (1969), *Four Essays on Liberty* (London: Oxford University Press).

Bonnett, M. (1986), 'Personal authenticity and public standards: towards the transcendence of a dualism', in Cooper, (1986), pp. 111–33.

Bourdieu, P. and Passeron, J. C. (1970), *La Réproduction* (Paris: Editions de Minuit), translated by R. Nice as *Reproduction in Education, Society and Culture* (London and Beverley Hills: Sage, 1977).

Bowles, S. and Gintis, H. (1976) *Schooling in Capitalist America* (London: Routledge & Kegan Paul).

Brown, S. C. (ed.) (1975), *Philosophers Discuss Education* (London: Macmillan).

Bruner, J. S. (1960), *The Process of Education* (New York: Random House).

Burgess, T. (ed.) (1986), *Education for Capability* (Windsor: NFER–Nelson).

Callaghan, J. (1976), Speech at Ruskin College, Oxford, 18 October, 1976, reported in *The Times Educational Supplement*, 22 October, 1976, pp. 1 and 72.

Carritt, E. F. (1947), *Ethical and Political Thinking* (Oxford: Clarendon Press).

Cooper, D. E. (1975), 'Quality and equality in education', in Brown (1975), 113–29.

Cooper, D. E. (1980), *Illusions of Equality* (London: Routledge & Kegan Paul).

Cooper, D. E. (1983), *Authenticity and Learning* (London: Routledge & Kegan Paul).

Cooper, D. E. (ed.) (1986), *Education, Values and Mind* (London: Routledge & Kegan Paul).

Cosin, B. R. (ed.) (1972), *Education Structure and Society* (Harmondsworth: Penguin).

Cranston, M. (1953), *Freedom: A New Analysis* (London: Longmans Green).

Crittenden, B. (1978), 'Autonomy as an aim of education', in Strike and Egan (1978), pp. 105–26.

Crosland, C. A. R. (1962), *The Conservative Enemy* (London: Cape).

Davies, I. K. (1976), *Objectives in Curriculum Design* (Maidenhead: McGraw Hill).

Dearden, R. F. (1972a), '"Needs" in education', in Dearden, Hirst and Peters (1972), pp. 50–64.

Dearden, R. F. (1972b), 'Education as a process of growth', in Dearden, Hirst and Peters (1972), pp. 65–84.

Dearden, R. F. (1972c), 'Happiness and education', in Dearden, Hirst and Peters (1972), pp. 95–112.

Dearden, R. F. (1972d), 'Autonomy and education', in Dearden, Hirst and Peters (1972), pp. 448–66.

Dearden, R. F. (1975), 'Autonomy as an educational ideal', in Brown (1975), pp. 3–18.

Dearden, R. F., Hirst, P. H. and Peters, R. S. (1972), *Education and the Development of Reason* (London: Routledge & Kegan Paul).

Degenhardt, M. A. B. (1976), 'Indoctrination', in Lloyd (1976), pp. 19–30.

Degenhardt, M. A. B. (1982), *Education and the Value of Knowledge* (London: Allen & Unwin).

Department of Education and Science (1985), *Education for All,* Swann Report (London: HMSO).

Dewey, J. (1916), *Democracy and Education* (New York: Macmillan, 1961).

Dewey, J. (1938) *Experience and Education,* New York: Collier, 1963.

Downey, M. and Kelly, A. V. (1978), *Moral Education, Theory and Practice* (London: Harper Row).

Doyle, J. F. (ed.) (1973), *Educational Judgements* (London: Routledge & Kegan Paul).

Durkheim, E. (1925), *L'Education Morale* (Paris: Alcan), translated as *Moral Education* (New York: Collier-Macmillan, 1961).

Dworkin: R. (1977), *Taking Rights Seriously* (London: Duckworth).

Elliott, R. K. (1975), 'Education and human being: I' in Brown (1975), pp. 45–72.

Elliott, R. K. (1977), 'Education and justification', *Proceedings of the Philosophy of Education Society of Great Britain,* vol. 11, pp. 7–27.

FEU (Further Education Curriculum Review and Development Unit) (1979), *A Basis for Choice* (London: HMSO).

Foot, P. (1967), 'Moral beliefs' in *Theories of Ethics* (London: Oxford University Press), pp. 83–100.

Gallie, W. B. (1955–6), 'Essentially contested concepts', *Proceedings of the Aristotelian Society,* vol. 56, pp. 167–98.

Gallop, G. and Dolan, J. (1981), 'Perspectives on the participation in sporting recreation amongst minority group youngsters', *Physical Education Review,* vol. 1, pp. 61–4.

Gewirth, A. (1973), 'Morality and autonomy in education', in Doyle (1973), pp. 33–45.

Gleeson, D. (ed.) (1977), *Identity and Structure* (Driffield: Nafferton Books).

Gleeson, D. (ed.) (1983), *Youth Training and the Search for Work* (London: Routledge & Kegan Paul).

Goldman, A. H. (1979), *Justice and Reverse Discrimination* (Princeton, NJ: Princeton University Press).

Griffiths, A. P. (1965), 'A deduction of universities', in Archambault (1965), pp. 187–208.

Handy, C. B. (1985), *Understanding Organisations* (Harmondsworth: Penguin).

Hargreaves, D. H. (1982), *The Challenge for the Comprehensive School* (London: Routledge & Kegan Paul).

Hartnett, A. and Naish, M. (eds.) (1976), *Theory and the Practice of Education,* Vol. 1 (London: Heinemann Educational Books).

Hirst, P. H. (1965), 'Liberal education and the nature of knowledge', in Archambault (1965), pp. 113–40.

Hirst, P. H. and Peters, R. S. (1970), *The Logic of Education* (London: Routledge & Kegan Paul).

Holt, J. (1977), *Instead of Education* (Harmondsworth: Penguin).

Honderich, T. (1976), *Three Essays on Political Violence* (Oxford: Blackwell).

Hooper, R. (ed.) (1971), *The Curriculum: Context, Design and Development* (Edinburgh: Oliver & Boyd).

Hume, D. (1751), *A Treatise of Human Nature,* ed. E. C. Mossner (Harmondsworth: Penguin, 1969).

Illich, I. (1971), *Deschooling Society* (London: Calder Boyars).

Jencks, C. (1975), *Inequality* (Harmondsworth: Penguin).

Jonathan, R. (1983), 'The manpower services model of education', *Cambridge Journal of Education,* vol. 13, no. 2, pp. 3–10.

Kibler, R. J., Barker L. L. and Miles, D. T. (1970), *Behavioural Objectives and Instruction* (Boston: Allyn & Bacon).

Kilpatrick, W. H. (1951), *Philosophy of Education* (New York and London: Macmillan).

Komisar, B. P. (1961), '"Need" and the needs, curriculum', in Smith and Ennis (1961), pp. 24–42.

Lloyd, D. I. (1976), *Philosophy and the Teacher* (London: Routledge & Kegan Paul).

Locke, J. (1689-90), *Two Treatises of Government,* ed. P. Laslett (Cambridge: Cambridge University Press, 1960).

MacIntyre, A. C. (1967), *A Short History of Ethics* (London: Routledge & Kegan Paul).

Mager, R. F. (1962), *Preparing Objectives for Programmed Instruction* (Belmont, Calif.: Fearon).

Manpower Services Commission (undated), *Training for Skills: A Programme for Action* (London: MSC).

Mardle, G. D. (1977), 'Power tradition and change: educational implications of the thought of Antonio Gramsci', in Gleeson (1977), pp. 134–52.

Maslow, A. (1954), *Motivation and Personality* (Chicago: Harper & Row).

Mill, J. S. (1859), *On Liberty* (London: Longmans Green, 1913).

Mill, J. S. (1861), 'Utilitarianism', in A. D. Lindsay (ed.), *Utilitarianism, Liberty, Representative Government* (London: Dent, 1910).

Mill, J. S. (1883), *The Subjection of Women* (London: Longmans Green).

Ministry of Education (1963), *Half Our Future* (London: HMSO).

Montefiore, A. (1979) 'Philosophy and moral and political education', *Journal of Philosophy of Education of Great Britain,* vol. 13, pp. 21–32.

Montessori, M. (1936), *The Secret of Childhood,* trans. B. B. Carter (London: Longman).

Naish, M. (1984), 'Education and essential contestability revisited', *Journal of Philosophy of Education of Great Britain,* vol. 18, 2, pp. 141–53.

Neill, A. S. (1962), *Summerhill: A Radical Approach to Education* (London: Gollancz).

Nozick, R. (1974), *Anarchy, State and Utopia* (Oxford: Blackwell).

Oakeshott, M. (1971), 'Education: the engagement and its frustration', *Proceedings of the Philosophy of Education Society of Great Britain,* vol. 5, no. 1, pp. 43–76.

O'Hear, A. (1981), *Education, Society and Human Nature* (London: Routledge & Kegan Paul).

Paine, T. (1791), *Rights of Man* (London: Dent, 1970).

Peters, R. S. (1964), *Education as Initiation* (London: Evans), reprinted in Peters (1973d), pp. 81-107.

Peters, R. S. (1966), *Ethics and Education* (London: Allen & Unwin).

Peters, R. S. (ed.) (1969), *Perspectives on Plowden* (London: Routledge & Kegan Paul).

Peters, R. S. (1970), 'Education and the educated man', *Proceedings of the Philosophy of Education Society of Great Britain,* vol. 4, pp. 5–20.

Peters, R. S. (ed.) (1973a), *The Philosophy of Education* (London: Oxford University Press).

Peters, R. S. (1973b), 'Aims of education – a conceptual enquiry', in Peters (1973a), pp. 11–57.

Peters, R. S. (1973c), 'The justification of education', in Peters (1973a), pp. 239–68.

Peters, R. S. (1973d), *Authority, Responsibility and Education* (London: Allen & Unwin).

Peters, R. S. (1973e), 'Must an educator have an aim?', in Peters (1973a), pp. 122–31.

Peters, R. S. (1974), *Psychology and Ethical Development* (London: Allen & Unwin).

Peters, R. S. (1977), *Education and the Education of Teachers* (London: Routledge & Kegan Paul).

Popham, W. J. (1970), 'Probing the validity of arguments against behavioural goals', in Kibler, Barker and Miles (1970), pp. 115–24.

Raphael, D. D. (1981), *Moral Philosophy* (Oxford: Oxford University Press).

Rawls, J. (1973), *A Theory of Justice* (London: Oxford University Press).

Rees, T. L. and Atkinson, P. (eds.) (1982), *Youth Unemployment and State Intervention* (London: Routledge & Kegan Paul).

Richards, J. R. (1980), *The Sceptical Feminist* (Harmondsworth: Penguin).

Rossi, A. (ed.) (1970), *Essays on Sex Equality* by John Stuart Mill and Harriet Taylor Mill (Chicago: University of Chicago Press).

Rousseau, J. J. (1762a), *Du Contrat Social,* published in English as *The Social Contract*, trans. G. D. H. Cole (London: Dent, 1913).

Rousseau, J. J. (1762b), *Emile*, trans. B. Foxley (London: Dent, 1911).

Russell, B. (1926), *On Education* (London: Allen & Unwin).

Rutter, M. and others (1979), *Fifteen Thousand Hours* (Shepton Mallet: Open Books).

Sarte, J. P. (1946) *L'Existentialisme est un Humanisme* (Paris: Editions de Minuit), translated as *Existentialism and Humanism* (London: Eyre Methuen, 1973).

Scheffler, I. (1962), *The Language of Education* (Springfield, Ill.: Thomas).

Smart, J. J. C. and Williams, B. (1973), *Utilitarianism: For and Against* (Cambridge: Cambridge University Press).

Smith, B. O. and Ennis, R. H. (1961), *Language and Concepts in Education* (Chicago: Rand McNally).

Snook, I. (1972), *Concepts of Indoctrination* (London: Routledge & Kegan Paul).

Sockett, H. T. (1972), 'Curriculum aims and objectives: taking a means to an end', *Proceedings of the Education Society of Great Britain,* vol. 6, no. 1, pp. 30–61.

Straughan, R. (1982), *Can We Teach Children to be Good?* (London: Allen & Unwin).

Straughan, R. and Wilson, J. (1983), *Philosophizing about Education* (London: Holt, Rinehart & Winston).

Strike, K. A. and Egan, K. (eds.) (1978), *Ethics and Educational Policy* (London: Routledge & Kegan Paul).

Trigg, R. (1985), *Understanding Social Science* (Oxford: Blackwell).

Vaizey, J. (1962), *Education for Tomorrow* (Harmondsworth: Penguin).

Warnock, G. J. (1967), *Contemporary Moral Philosophy* (London: Macmillan).

Warnock, M. (1967) *Existentialist Ethics* (London: Macmillan).

Warnock, M. (1977), *Schools of Thought* (London: Faber & Faber).

White, A. (1974), 'Needs and wants', *Proceedings of the Philosophy of Education Society of Great Britain,* vol. 8 no. 2, pp. 159–80.

White, J. P. (1970), 'Indoctrination; reply to I. M. M. Gregory and R. G. Woods', *Proceedings of the Philosophy of Education Society of Great Britain,* vol. 4, pp. 107–20.

White, J. P. (1973), *Towards a Compulsory Curriculum* (London: Routledge & Kegan Paul).

White, J. (1978), 'The aims of education: three legacies of the British idealists', *Journal of Philosophy of Education,* 12, pp. 5–12.

White, J. P. (1982), *The Aims of Education Restated* (London: Routledge & Kegan Paul).

White, J. and Gordon, P. (1979), *Philosophers as Educational Reformers* (London: Routledge & Kegan Paul).

White, P. (1972), 'Socialization and education', in Dearden, Hirst and Peters (1972), pp. 113–31.

Whitehead, A. N. (1929), *The Aims of Education* (London: Benn, 1962).

Willey, R. (1984), *Race, Equality and Schools* (London: Methuen).

Williams, B. (1972), *Morality* (Cambridge: Cambridge University Press).

Willis, P. (1977), *Learning to Labour* (Guildford: Saxon House).

Wilson, B. (ed.) (1974), *Rationality* (Oxford: Blackwell).

Wilson, J. (1979), *Preface to the Philosophy of Education* (London: Routledge & Kegan Paul).

Wilson, J. (1986), 'Race, culture and education: some conceptual problems', *Oxford Review of Education,* vol. 12, pp. 3–15.

Wilson, J. and Cowell, B. (1983), 'The democratic myth', *Journal of Philosophy of Education,* vol. 17, no. 1, pp. 111–17.

Wilson, J., Williams, N. and Sugarman, B. (1967), *Introduction to Moral Education* (Harmondsworth: Penguin).

Wilson, P. S. (1971), *Interest and Discipline in Education* (London: Routledge & Kegan Paul).

Winch, P. (1958), *The Idea of a Social Science* (London: Routledge & Kegan Paul).

Wringe, C. A. (1981a), 'Education, schooling and the world of work', *British Journal of Educational Studies,* vol. 19, no. 2, pp. 123–37.

Wringe, C. A. (1981b), *Children's Rights: A Philosophical Study* (London: Routledge & Kegan Paul).

Wringe, C. A. (1984), *Democracy, Schooling and Political Education* (London: Allen & Unwin).

Young, M. F. D. (ed.) (1971), *Knowledge and Control* (London: Collier-Macmillan).

Zec, P. (1980), 'Multicultural education: what kind of relativism is possible?', *Journal of Philosophy of Education,* vol. 14, no. 1, pp. 77–86.

Index

151

Also from Unwin Hyman

MIXED ABILITY GROUPING: A PHILOSOPHICAL PERSPECTIVE
Charles Bailey and David Bridges

TEACHING ART TO YOUNG CHILDREN 4–9
Rob Barnes

FEELING AND REASON IN THE ARTS
David Best

MEANS AND ENDS IN EDUCATION
Brenda Cohen

EDUCATION AND THE VALUE OF KNOWLEDGE
M. A. B. Degenhardt

THE EDUCATION OF FEELING AND EMOTION
Francis Dunlop

QUESTIONS IN AESTHETIC EDUCATION
H. B. Redfern

RELIGIOUS EDUCATION: PHILOSOPHICAL PERSPECTIVES
John Sealey

FREEDOM AND DISCIPLINE
Richard Smith

CAN WE TEACH CHILDREN TO BE GOOD?
Roger Straughan

THE BEHAVIOURIST IN THE CLASSROOM
Edited by Kevin Wheldall

DEMOCRACY, SCHOOLING AND POLITICAL EDUCATION
Colin Wringe